# INFLUENCER

The influential are no longer only those with celebrity status—but until now there has been no authoritative resource on the theory and practice of influencer marketing. This book will educate and inspire decision makers, researchers, students, and influencers themselves.

Diving deeper than the many "how-to" books on the influencer phenomenon, this book brings in frameworks from marketing, sociology, psychology, and communication studies to redefine the influencer as a persona (related to a person, group of people, or organization) that possesses greater than average sway over others. Cornwell and Katz go on to:

- introduce the influencers, macro and nano, authentic and inauthentic, ascending and fading;
- consider their relationship with brands in the marketing ecosystem, along with the regulations that set limits on influencer marketing;
- describe how influence is measured and evaluated and look into the future; and
- bring together the latest research on influencer marketing and organize it for the reader.

The book serves both those who want to understand the science behind influencer marketing and those who want to most effectively employ influencers in brand strategy. Instructors, students, and professionals will appreciate the international examples from multiple industries applying theories to the real world.

**T. Bettina Cornwell** is Professor of Marketing and the Philip H. Knight Chair in the Lundquist College of Business at the University of Oregon. She also serves as Head of the Department of Marketing. She is known for her research in marketing communications and for her work at the intersection of marketing and public policy.

In addition to academic research, Cornwell works with companies and non-profits on branding and communication strategy. The second edition of her book, *Sponsorship in Marketing: Effective Partnerships in Sports, Arts and Events* was published with Routledge in 2020.

Cornwell's Ph.D. in marketing, with a minor in cognitive psychology, is from The University of Texas, Austin, as is her MBA with an emphasis on international business. Her B.A., also in business, is from Florida State University.

**Helen Katz** is Senior Vice President, Global Research Lead in the Data Sciences Practice of Publicis Media. She is a trusted industry expert on research, with a particular focus on data quality and reliable measurement.

Katz has served in various strategic research capacities within Publicis Groupe. She started her industry career at DDB Needham. She has also worked in academia, beginning as an advertising professor at Michigan State University. Currently, she is an adjunct professor at DePaul University. She has published three textbooks on advertising and media, the most recent of which is *The Media Handbook* (7th edition, 2019).

Katz has a Ph.D. in Communications and an M.S. in Advertising from the University of Illinois, and a B.A. in English Language & Literature from the University of London.

# INFLUENCER

## The Science Behind
## Swaying Others

*T. Bettina Cornwell and Helen Katz*

Routledge
Taylor & Francis Group

NEW YORK AND LONDON

First published 2021
by Routledge
52 Vanderbilt Avenue, New York, NY 10017

and by Routledge
2 Park Square, Milton Park, Abingdon, Oxon, OX14 4RN

*Routledge is an imprint of the Taylor & Francis Group, an Informa business*

*Library of Congress Cataloging-in-Publication Data*
A catalog record for this book has been requested

ISBN: 978-0-367-48116-2 (hbk)
ISBN: 978-0-367-46849-1 (pbk)
ISBN: 978-1-003-03776-7 (ebk)

DOI: 10.4324/9781003037767

# CONTENTS

# ABOUT THE AUTHORS

**T. Bettina Cornwell** (Ph.D. in marketing, The University of Texas) is the Philip H. Knight Chair in the Lundquist College of Business at the University of Oregon. She also serves as Head of the Department of Marketing. Her research focuses on marketing communications and consumer behavior and often includes international and public policy emphases.

Bettina's research has appeared in the *Academy of Management Review, Journal of Advertising, Journal of Consumer Research, Journal of Experimental Psychology: Applied, Journal of the Academy of Marketing Science*, and *Journal of Marketing*. The second edition of her book, *Sponsorship in Marketing: Effective Partnerships in Sports, Arts and Events* was published with Routledge in 2020.

She was the 2016 Thomas C. Stewart Distinguished Professor at the Lundquist College of Business. Together with a previous Ph.D. student, she received the best paper of the year in the *Journal of Consumer Affairs* in 2017. With co-authors writing in the *Journal of Marketing*, she received the best paper award from the American Marketing Association Sports and Sponsorship-Linked Marketing Special Interest Group (2018), and, with co-authors, the Nickerson Award for the best paper in the *Journal of Experimental Psychology: Applied* (2019).

**Helen Katz** (Ph.D. in communications, University of Illinois at Urbana-Champaign) is Senior Vice President, Global Research Lead in the Data Sciences Practice of Publicis Media. She is a trusted industry expert on research, with a particular focus on data quality and reliable measurement. Her interest in innovation inspired her to play an instrumental role in developing the best practices in the measurement of addressable TV and advanced video campaigns in the U.S.

A 19-year Publicis Groupe veteran, Katz has served in various strategic research capacities for Publicis Media, Starcom, Zenith, and GM Planworks—the holding company's former division devoted to the General Motors business. In 2009, she was integral to the Publicis Groupe team that launched The Pool—a unique research consortium that aimed to identify the next new ad formats across various channels such as online video, mobile/tablets, and more. Prior to joining Publicis Groupe, she was Vice President, Media Research Manager at DDB Needham.

She began her career as an advertising professor at Michigan State University, and is currently an adjunct professor at DePaul University. Helen's research has appeared in *Admap, Journal of Advertising Research, Journal of Current Issues in Research on Advertising*, and *Journal of Interactive Advertising*, among others. She has published three textbooks on advertising and media, the most recent of which is *The Media Handbook* (7th edition, 2019). She serves on the Accrediting Committee of the Accrediting Council on Education in Journalism and Mass Communications (ACEJMC) and is the ex officio Chair of the Executive Committee of the Media Rating Council. Katz is also the recipient of the Advertising Research Foundation's "Great Minds" award for research innovation, Jay Chiat's Strategic Excellence Silver Award for innovation, and Stars of Attribution leadership award.

Katz has an M.S. in Advertising from the University of Illinois and a B.A. in English Language & Literature from the University of London.

# FOREWORD

Influence is a strange thing. What influenced us to write this book? Why do we listen to or watch some individuals we never met when they are promoting brands we might know? How does influencer marketing really work, when you look behind the number of likes or followers or shares or tweets?

It was questions like this that drew us together to write this book, though like many of the strongest brand relationships, ours goes back much further to one summer when Bettina visited as an academic fellow at the ad agency where Helen worked. The friendship that we developed years ago in Chicago has lasted, despite sometimes considerable geographic distances. We swap stories of both our professional and family experiences, while still pursuing our divergent career paths. What has never changed is our mutual curiosity for the marketing and advertising world in which we each live. Whether it is Bettina's passion for understanding sponsorship marketing or Helen's interest in studying how and why people use media, both of us are driven by a need to explore and explain. Influencers have become a huge part of both our worlds, and we needed to chronicle their ascendance and be better able to envision their future.

When we first discussed this book, it was our differences and similarities that attracted us each to the project. How could we explain influencer marketing from both a theoretical and conceptual standpoint and a practitioner viewpoint? That remained our goal as we drafted chapters, swapped those back and forth, and talked through the areas where we had differing perspectives. We believe the result is a unique combination of practical examples and academic explanations to help readers learn more about influencers and influencer marketing.

We could not have completed this project without the help and support of numerous people. Our editor, Meredith Norwich, provided the enthusiasm for the project and ensured that we stayed on track, through both the writing and the production stages. Amy Nuetzman at the University of Oregon gave us invaluable help when it came to proofing our final drafts after we were both too jaded to spot inconsistencies or sentences that no longer made sense. Our families were also crucial supporters of this endeavor. For Helen, special gratitude to her husband Eric and daughters Stephanie, Caroline, and Vanessa, whose collective enthusiasm and unbounded support inspire and influence her every day. For Bettina, unending appreciation for the home team of Steve, David, Luke, Robert, and, our mascot Comma, our mini long-hair dachshund.

# 1

# INTRODUCTION TO INFLUENCERS

It is 7 am on a Monday morning. Your phone alarm beeps to wake you up. You lie in the bed and check your social media accounts . . . Instagram, Facebook, Twitter. Pretty soon, you realize it is 7:30 am and you'll be late to work if you don't hurry. Once out the door, you pop in your Air Pods and listen to your Spotify playlist, which helps you ignore the crowded subway. During the day in the office, you peek pretty regularly at your social media apps on the phone to make sure you are keeping up with the news, as well as your friends' posts. A daily news podcast accompanies you home, and after a quick ready-to-eat dinner, you settle down to watch your new favorite streamed show on Hulu or Amazon Prime Video or Netflix. That also gives you some time to respond to some posts and text friends and family about the next weekend's plans. Before you turn out the lights, you watch a few funny BuzzFeed and TikTok videos and then listen to your meditation app, the combination of which leaves you relaxed and ready to sleep.

Sounds familiar at all?

Now let's rewind, and think about that day when you were likely exposed to brand messages from Instagram, Facebook, Twitter, and maybe Spotify as well (unless you shelled out for premium, ad-free music). Also think about the posters in subway platforms, trains, escalator; elevator ads in the office; podcast sponsors; Hulu ads before and during your favorite programs; brand mentions in Netflix content; BuzzFeed, and, last but not the least, TikTok.

The estimates of how many ads or brand messages an average consumer is exposed to on a daily basis vary tremendously. Some say

DOI: 10.4324/9781003037767-1

it is as high as 3,000 times a day! What all these marketers want to do is try to influence you, as the consumer, in some way or other—to be aware of their product, prefer it, want it (and search for it), and to talk about it with others. Ultimately, they want you to buy it and use it (and buy it again). This notion of influence is not new. It was what Lydia Pinkham's Compound was trying to do in some of the earliest newspaper ad messages in the 1870s. It was why Coca-Cola became an official Olympics sponsor starting in 1928. And it was what Procter & Gamble's intent was in sponsoring the first television soap operas in the 1940s.

Today's version of influence is, in many ways, very different. Celebrities, like Kim Kardashian, use their fame and personality to influence millions of people to buy FitTea and SugarBearHair products. Regular people, like Gretchen Geraghty, are helping brands such as CVS Pharmacy, Fabletics, and Care/of Vitamins by using their influence to persuade millions like them of the best health and wellness products. During the coronavirus pandemic of 2020, even organizations became influencers. The World Health Organization (WHO) created and distributed numerous videos encouraging people to wash their hands and explaining how to do it effectively, garnering millions of followers and likes in the process. Here, we begin our discussion with influencers as defined by the Word of Mouth Marketing Association: "A person or group of people who possess greater than average potential to influence due to attributes such as frequency of communication, personal persuasiveness or size of and centrality to a social network, among others."[1]

Why do they matter? How are influencers any different from earlier methods used to persuade customers to buy a certain brand of toothpaste or cereal or car? How have influencers altered the relationship between consumers and the brands they buy or the media they use? This chapter considers the history of influencer marketing. While it seems like a new phenomenon, its roots can in fact be traced back several decades.

Once we establish the foundations of influencer marketing, we dive deeper into the role of influencers in the broader marketing ecosystem (Chapter 2), investigate the boundaries between endorsers and influencers (Chapter 3), explore the process model for influencers (Chapter 4), examine the fledgling regulatory system surrounding influencer marketing (Chapter 5), note barriers and challenges to consider (Chapter 6), explain how influence can be measured (Chapter 7), and, finally, look at what the future holds for influencer marketing (Chapter 8).

## The Foundations of Influencer Marketing

Before there was influencer marketing, brands relied on two key forms of external motivation to persuade consumers to buy their products. The first was celebrity marketing, and the second was word of mouth. Celebrity marketing, as noted earlier, dates back many decades. The idea that people respond positively to a product or service if someone famous talks about it is founded on plenty of psychological research on the power of authority in persuasion.[2]

Newspapers in the early 20th century featured famous sports figures such as Cy Young and Babe Ruth promoting tobacco products and actress Lilly Langtry endorsing Pears soap. The phenomenon continued throughout the 20th century, led largely by the big tobacco companies that hired a slew of famous actors and actresses, from Ronald Reagan and Marlene Dietrich to Gary Cooper and Barbara Stanwyck, to promote their cigarettes. With the growth of radio, these same companies started to sponsor programs, such as the Lucky Strike Dance Hour, during which radio listeners heard the brand mentioned nearly every 30 seconds!

While the early years of television were more about putting the brand name in the program title, such as Kraft Television Theater or Colgate Comedy Hour, it was not long before celebrities were appearing on the brands' behalf in 60-second TV commercials. Lucille Ball appeared in ads for Summerettes shoes, Rita Hayworth promoted Max Factor cosmetics, and John Cameron Swayze was seen in ads for Timex watches. During the last several decades of the 20th century, it was hard to watch TV without seeing famous faces appear during the commercial breaks, such as those of Farrah Fawcett, Michael Jordan, Tiger Woods, or Muhammad Ali. The list seemed endless.

While brands have often turned to celebrities to support their message and promote their image in advertisements, they have also always been eager to generate positive word of mouth from regular individuals. The notion that people respond more positively to things that have been endorsed by friends and family has a lengthy heritage in the psychological literature.[3] Informally, companies have long known that when customers had a positive experience and spoke to others about it, their businesses grew. The growth of word-of-mouth marketing, however, is said to have formally started in the 1970s, thanks to a psychologist named George Silverman, who realized while conducting focus groups with physicians that the positive opinions of one doctor helped change the opinions of the others.[4]

It is inherently difficult for brands to force consumers to talk about them positively, so some of the best examples have occurred when the company did little to create the buzz (at least initially). Companies such as Apple, Starbucks, and Zappos have all grown their businesses, in part, by getting their satisfied customers to not only remain loyal to them but also speak favorably about them to others. One of the best examples of the power of word of mouth, however, is in the nonprofit world. Here, the charity working to find a cure for Amyotrophic Lateral Sclerosis (ALS) created an enormous phenomenon, both online and offline, in what became known as the Ice Bucket Challenge.[5] People were challenged by friends to dump a bucket of ice water over their heads within 24 hours (and share online) or else donate $1 to the ALS Foundation. The campaign raised more than $100 million in donations, along with a huge enhancement in the awareness of the disease.

That campaign not only marked the enormous power of word-of-mouth marketing (and, to a lesser extent, the power of celebrity endorsers as many famous people joined in), but more importantly, it also demonstrated the critical importance of the Internet and social media in driving the success of a brand.

The subsequent rise of influencer marketing is in fact inextricably linked to the phenomenon of sharing, and, to some degree, liking. Shared information such as word-of-mouth communication has always been of interest in marketing[6] and consumer behavior.[7] The Internet, however, has amplified the number of individuals any one person might reach. "Liking" a brand by clicking an icon of approval (e.g., a heart or smiling face) has allowed marketers to gauge affinity for their brand or brand-related communications.[8]

It is quite staggering to consider how large the sharing phenomenon is, with more than 200 million people in the U.S. using social networks, a number that gets magnified rapidly when global usage is considered, rising to nearly 3 billion. Facebook alone is estimated to have 1.7 billion users around the world, with both Instagram and WeChat moving toward 1 billion each. According to the survey company GlobalWebIndex, about one-quarter of social media users say they turn to these outlets in order "to share my opinion," while about the same percentage do so because "many of my friends are on them."[9] This combination perhaps helps to explain the growth of influencer marketing, which we explore further in Chapter 2.

## Definitional Development

In order to discuss "influencer marketing," we need to start with a definition of marketing. This exploration of definitions of marketing also leads to a new, slightly different definition of influencer. The American Marketing Association (AMA) explains that "Marketing is the activity, set of institutions, and processes for creating, communicating, delivering, and exchanging offerings that have value for customers, clients, partners, and society at large."[10]

This definition of marketing has become broad-based and more inclusive over time. Importantly, marketing is for nonprofit as well as for-profit organizations, products, as well as ideas, and can be employed for good as well as evil (e.g., in propaganda). It can be employed in the health sector to encourage people to get a vaccine, in charities to gain donations, or in political campaigns to bring in the votes. "Influencer marketing" has been described as a "brand collaborating with an online influencer to market one of its products or services."[11] Considering the breadth of entities that might utilize marketing, this definition is somewhat narrow.

## Definitional Breadth

Early public relations researchers described social media influencers as a "type of independent third-party endorsers who shape audience attitudes through blogs, tweets, and the use of other social media."[12] Their orientation was toward individuals who give advice or provide commentary on products or services. In the early 2000s, the influencers of social media had not yet developed.

Influencers have evolved, as did spokespeople decades before, to include cartoon characters, animals, or company CEOs. It is essential to think broadly about the potential of a variety of influencers. Admittedly, behind their projected personas, there are real people, at times even a team of them.

---

### THE FIRST INSECT INFLUENCER[13]

At first, it seems audacious to hear: "My name is B and I want to become a famous influencer" as it states on bee_nfluencer's Instagram account. When the next two statements are "The more you will follow me, the more brands will pay to work with me" and "All the money I make will finance bee preservation," the tone changes. As a tiny insect socialite, bee_nfluencer was created in 2019 by Fondation de France to raise funds to save bees from possible extinction. B is a fashion icon and is in a meaningful relationship with bumble_fit, her yoga instructor. She hangs out in "beestros" on the weekend; and she takes the time to educate her followers on her community by, for example, explaining the difference between the ways honeybees and wild bees stay warm in winter. Her work with @fondationdefrance includes projects such as the one on improving agricultural ecosystems to support bee health. She always emphasizes that no one is too small to make a difference.

Pet influencers such as Buddy and Boo have had 16 million followers on Facebook and another 582,000 on Instagram.[14] People might also be familiar with Swaggy, a male Husky with signature pink ears from TikTok. Others might recall Grumpy Cat, who, before her death in May 2019, had nearly two million Instagram followers, and, to this day, has hundreds of memes shared widely on social media.

It should also be accepted that the degree of influence varies greatly and that it ebbs and flows. Some people, with several million followers, are considered to be macro influencers (Kylie Jenner, Selena Gomez, or Huda Kattan). They can easily command more than $1 million per post. Then there are micro influencers, more often regular people who have gained a following through their expertise or passion on a topic. Finally, we have nano influencers, with much smaller followings but often a niche interest that makes them extremely persuasive to those who follow them. We will explore these influencer types in subsequent chapters.

The term "influencer," as we now think of it, only entered dictionary. com in 2016.[15] This addition followed a surge of searches for the term, which began in 2015. The definition is as follows:

**Noun**

- a person or thing that influences: The most powerful influencer of beliefs is direct experience.
- a person who has the power to influence many people, as through social media or traditional media: Companies look for Facebook influencers who can promote their brands.

For an influencer on social media to correspond to a single individual flies in the face of how social media works on a day-to-day basis. For example, most social media managers not only tend accounts for other individuals or organizations but also have their own personal accounts. Their job may be developing the persona for a brand or company, but they are also potentially social media influencers in their own right.

One key point developed here is that influencers are personas, playing roles or characters that they present to others. This may be authentically close to the person or entity or may be largely fictional. As noted earlier, it is not the number of individuals that they influence, but their potential for persuasiveness with their selected audience (large or small) that makes them an influencer. At times the fiction is accepted, especially if the audience is brought into the fiction and knows it as such. When, however, audiences are duped, repercussions can be expected. When it was disclosed by her landlord that the luxury influencer, Lisa Li, was in fact living in foul conditions with garbage and animal excrement everywhere, her ability to effectively promote a luxury lifestyle quickly deteriorated and she had to apologize to her million followers.[16]

## Redefining Influencer

With all of the previous points in mind, we must return to the opening definition of an influencer and modify it to encompass all the personas and all the products, services, causes, and ideas they influence. Adapted from the Word of Mouth Association's definition:

> An influencer is a persona (related to a person, group of people, or organization) that possesses greater than average potential to sway others in terms of thoughts, attitudes and behaviors due to attributes of their communication frequency, persuasiveness, social network or other characteristics.

One might then ask, could a brand be an influencer? Brands such as Patagonia and one of their distributors, REI, have been known for years for their anti-consumption campaigns such as "don't buy this jacket" and #OptOutside instead of shopping on Black Friday. Patagonia also sewed "Vote the a-holes out" into clothing to make a statement on the importance of elected officials in altering the course of climate change. These anti-consumption and pro-environmental messages could be viewed cynically as greenwashing, but brands have the power to shift consumer attitudes on a topic not related to selling their brands.[17] While these are examples of influence and they involve the marketing of an idea, they are not examples of influencer marketing.

Influencer marketing has been described this way:

> By involving influencers (e.g., by offering to test a product, orga-nizing an exclusive event, . . . or simply paying them), brands aim to stimulate influencers to endorse their products and this way build up their image among influencers' often huge base of fol-lowers, a practice that is called influencer marketing.[18]

Thus, "influencer marketing" is marketing activities (as previously defined) that employ personas. The move to utilize the term "persona" is also in keeping with conceptual research on influencers.[19, 20] As well, it is a common objective that a definition should match the breadth of the phenomenon being defined.

There is certainly some luck behind the success of many people who gain fame and fortune as influencers, and it does not always last. But, as we will show in subsequent chapters, an understanding of the science behind swaying others will help both brands and researchers see how influencers fit in the marketing ecosystem and in consumer behavior. Likewise, consumers can become more informed about how they may be being influenced.

## Discussion Questions

1. Think about all the ads you were exposed to anywhere in the past week. How many of them included a celebrity or an influencer? Do you think you remembered them more than other marketing messages that did not have any influencer? Why or why not?
2. How many social media platforms do you currently use? How much time do you spend on each per day? In that time, how much content are you creating and posting yourself? How much content are you sharing with others (reposting, retweeting, etc.), which you see on social media platforms?
3. Has your use of social media changed at all in the past 6–12 months? If yes, please clarify why?
4. Brands are interested in having control of content and therefore are interested in avatar influencers, as animated graphical representations of personas. What are the advantages and disadvantages of using avatars and will this change over time?

## Notes

1. www.aaaa.org/index.php?checkfileaccess=/wp-content/uploads/legacy-pdfs/WOMMA-%20Influencer%20Guidebook%20-%202013-05.pdf
2. Cialdini, R. B. (2001). The science of persuasion. *Scientific American, 284*(2), 76–81.
3. Duhan, D. F., Johnson, S. D., Wilcox, J. B., & Harrell, G. D. (1997). Influences on consumer use of word-of-mouth recommendation sources. *Journal of the Academy of Marketing Science, 25*(4), 283.
4. Silverman, G. (2011). *Secrets of word-of-mouth marketing: How to trigger exponential sales through runaway word of mouth.* New York: Amacom Books.
5. Pressgrove, G., McKeever, B. W., & Jang, S. M. (2018). What is contagious? Exploring why content goes viral on Twitter: A case study of the ALS ice bucket challenge. *International Journal of Nonprofit and Voluntary Sector Marketing, 23*(1), e1586.
6. De Matos, C. A., & Rossi, C. A. V. (2008). Word-of-mouth communications in marketing: A meta-analytic review of the antecedents and moderators. *Journal of the Academy of Marketing Science, 36*(4), 578–596.
7. Berger, J. (2014). Word of mouth and interpersonal communication: A review and directions for future research. *Journal of Consumer Psychology, 24*(4), 586–607.

8. Lipsman, A., Mudd, G., Rich, M., & Bruich, S. (2012). The power of "like": How brands reach (and influence) fans through social-media marketing. *Journal of Advertising Research, 52*(1), 40–52.

9. GlobalWebIndex, 2020.

10. www.ama.org/the-definition-of-marketing-what-is-marketing/

11. https://influencermarketinghub.com/what-is-influencer-marketing/

12. Freberg, K., Graham, K., McGaughey, K., & Freberg, L. A. (2011). Who are the social media influencers? A study of public perceptions of personality. *Public Relations Review, 37*, 90–92.

13 www.designboom.com/design/bee-influencer-instagram-save-the-bees-11-04-2019/

14. https://socialbook.io/blog/top-30-pet-influencers-most-popular-animals-on-social-media/

15. www.dictionary.com/e/influencer/

16. https://nypost.com/2019/09/26/luxury-influencers-nasty-apartment-exposed-by-landlord/

17. www.wri.org/blog/2018/02/dont-read-article-how-ads-against-consumerism-help-sustainability

18. De Veirman, M., Cauberghe, V., & Hudders, L. (2017). Marketing through Instagram influencers: The impact of number of followers and product divergence on brand attitude. *International Journal of Advertising, 36*(5), 798–828, 801.

19. Childers, C. C., Lemon, L. L., & Hoy, M. G. (2019). # Sponsored# Ad: Agency perspective on influencer marketing campaigns. *Journal of Current Issues & Research in Advertising, 40*(3), 258–274.

20. Campbell, C., & Farrell, J. R. (2020). More than meets the eye: The functional components underlying influencer marketing. *Business Horizons, 63*, 469–479.

## Further Reading

Kadekova, Z., & Holienčinová, M. (2018). Influencer marketing as a modern phenomenon creating a new frontier of virtual opportunities. *Communication Today, 9*(2).

Kemp, A., Randon McDougal, E., & Syrdal, H. (2019). The matchmaking activity: An experiential learning exercise on influencer marketing for the digital marketing classroom. *Journal of Marketing Education, 41*(2), 141–153.

Kim, M., & Lee, M. (2017). Brand-related user-generated content on social media: The roles of source and sponsorship. *Internet Research, 27*(5), 1085–1103.

# 2

# INFLUENCERS IN THE MARKETING ECOSYSTEM

Many treat marketing influencers as if they are somehow separate from the larger advertising and marketing ecosystem; they are, in fact, firmly embedded within it. Although there are still discussions about exactly where influencers fit, there should no longer be any doubt that their role does lie within the marketing domain. This chapter examines that larger environment, noting the heritage of influencer marketing, as well as how and where it overlaps with older forms of media and communication to link brands to consumers.

If you open your Instagram app and see a video of Emily Henderson talking about her love of FabFitFun, it is all too easy to think that this is happening in isolation, and that the connection between influencer and brand happened fortuitously because Henderson just happened to enjoy the subscription box service and wanted to talk about it. However, behind her influential posts and brand mentions lies a much bigger strategic plan, a vision for how this brand wants to reach its target audience and communicate its message that, for a subscription price, each member will receive a quarterly box full of premium products.

When Chris Burkard, a popular and influential travel photographer with nearly three million Instagram followers, works with brands such as Keen or Patagonia, there is certainly an overt connection for people to make (rugged footwear and clothing, suitable for travel to extreme places). Yet these companies are doing far more than influencer marketing. Patagonia, for example, spent close to $10 million on its advertising in 2018, placing its messages on local television, newspapers, digital display, and mobile, among other media.

DOI: 10.4324/9781003037767-2

## Marketing, Advertising, and Media

So, let's start with a brief overview of how marketing, advertising, and media fit together. The long-standing purpose of marketing is a means to help sell a product or service. Advertising is one way to do that, as part of the promotional efforts that a company uses. Within advertising, marketers turn to diverse kinds of media to convey their brand messages. However, marketing involves much more than advertising. It also requires a consideration of the product itself, the right pricing strategy, and distribution channels. The focus of advertising is to develop the optimal strategy to sell the brand, along with the creative messages that will resonate most with the audience, persuading them to purchase that specific brand rather than its competitors. How, where, and when the message is conveyed is determined by those working in media.

A common way to analyze the many media options is to subdivide them into paid, owned, and earned.[1] Paid media refer to the channels where an advertiser buys space or time to place the message, such as television, radio, magazines, newspapers, outdoor billboards, and digital media. Owned media include the diverse channels that the brand owns outright (such as its website), along with those where it can pay to get an ownership right, such as sponsorship or content integration. Earned media offer brands opportunities to earn the trust of the consumer, whether through social media liking and sharing or through the more traditional route of word of mouth (i.e., discussing a brand with friends and family).

## Paid Media

The first advertisements to appear in media were in newspapers, back in the 18th century in England. In the U.S., newspapers also started to incorporate ads from early on, as a means of generating revenue to help pay to print the newspaper. Indeed, most forms of paid media help to subsidize the cost of the content that people are consuming, whether that is in television, radio, or magazines. The one exception here is outdoor billboards where the primary purpose is to deliver an advertiser's message. Here is a brief overview of each paid media form, in terms of both consumer use and advertising spend. Note that most of the data that follow are from the U.S. only, with reference to other countries where applicable.

### Television

The U.S. television advertising market is enormous and, despite the ongoing and rapid changes in how people watch TV (decreasingly live when it airs on a TV set and increasingly through streaming services viewed on multiple devices on demand), television is still a healthy medium for advertisers and consumers. The average U.S. household is reported to watch 8 hours of TV per day, according to Nielsen. That equates to about 5 hours per day for the average adult. Advertisers spend anywhere from a few hundred dollars to place a 30-second TV commercial on a local station to more than $5 million to appear in the annual Super Bowl football game. Each year, about $70 billion is spent on television, whether nationally or locally. National TV includes the "Big 4" broadcast networks (ABC, CBS, FOX, and NBC) as well as myriad more niche-oriented cable channels (ESPN for sports, CNN for news, etc.). Local TV involves placing ad messages on the local TV affiliates of the broadcast networks (WABC in New York and KCBS in Los Angeles). The television advertising marketplace operates primarily as a supply-and-demand one. That is, there is a finite amount of commercial time available to sell (even though it continues to expand year by year, so that in an average hour of primetime TV, there are upwards of 16 minutes of commercials). The demand for that time has not dropped significantly over the years as advertisers have moved dollars to digital, which means that even as the audiences for TV shows get smaller, the cost for commercial time does not go down by that amount.

In the U.S., the cost for national TV ads is based on the rating of the program in which that ad will appear. A rating represents the percentage of the population (or defined target audience) that is viewing a program. If the rating is higher, the exposure for the ad and therefore the cost of the ad time will also be higher. In the heyday of TV, when viewers had only three TV networks from which to choose, a top-rated program could be viewed by more than half of all U.S. households. Today, the typical primetime rating is somewhere between a 2 and a 3. This means, for example, that 2 percent of adults aged 18–49 years watched *This Is Us* on a given Thursday on NBC, or 3 percent of men aged 25–54 years watched *Sunday Night Football* on CBS.

TV planning and buying are in many ways stuck with legacy approaches that were first introduced more than 50 years ago. That is, the medium is thought of in terms of dayparts, such as Primetime or Daytime, and formats, such as Situation Comedies or Dramas. Ratings are calculated primarily for broad age and gender groups, based on the average commercial rating of the live airing plus 3 days of time-shifted viewing (national) or 7 days in the case of local (spot) TV.

Those ratings are compiled and reported by Nielsen, which operates a panel of 45,000 homes that are nationally representative of the total U.S. population.[2] The people in those households agree to have their TV sets monitored to tell Nielsen what channels are being viewed, as well as to push buttons on a special remote control "people meter" to identify (by age and gender) who is viewing each time they start and stop watching TV. Nielsen has started to supplement this approach by using second-by-second tuning from set top boxes and smart TV data or modeling the viewing in smaller markets from that occurring nationally. The set top box (sometimes called Return-Path Data, or RPD) is the primary data source for another audience measurement company, Comscore, offering more expansive and more granular data, collecting TV tuning from 30 million homes, but this approach does not identify who is viewing. A third approach to measurement is offered by several companies such as Inscape and Samba TV, who pull back all the tuning data from smart (Internet-connected) TV sets and then use Automatic Content Recognition (ACR) to determine what is on the screen at that time. This, too, is more granular and at a greater scale, but without the person-level identification.

As noted in Chapter 1, many of the early television ads featured celebrities who would talk favorably about the brands they were help-ing to promote (for a fee). Elizabeth Taylor and Humphrey Bogart helped promote Whitman's Sampler box of chocolates, while Alfred Hitchcock promoted Western Union telegrams. These celebrity endors-ers are in some ways the forerunners of today's influencers, since they too were paid by brands to promote them through the media. Brands were also key to the development of television programs. Indeed, the reason that the term "soap opera" was created was that companies that sold detergents, such as Procter & Gamble, helped fund the development of those programs. Companies such as Kraft and Philco had their names included in the programs, such as the Kraft Television Theatre and Philco Television Playhouse. This remained a popular practice through the 1950s, before brands moved their marketing dol-lars into 60-second TV commercials, giving them the opportunity to promote their messages in a concentrated timeframe.

## Radio

During an average week, nearly all (92 percent) of the U.S. population is reached by radio, according to Nielsen.[3] That figure has been stable for decades, as has the amount of time that people spend listening to radio or, more accurately, audio. Just as television viewing patterns have shifted away from a family sitting around one television set watch-ing the same program at the same time, so has radio listening become more personalized. The growth of digital forms of audio, whether a radio station that can be heard online or pureplay audio services such as Spotify or Apple Music, has transformed this legacy medium.

Traditional radio, like traditional TV, is measured by Nielsen Audio through broad demographic (age/gender) ratings that can show for every quarter-hour period what percent of a target group was listening to which radio station. In contrast to television, where most ad dollars are spent nationally, radio is considered a local medium. People listen to B96 in Chicago or WWWQ in Atlanta. Stations are defined by their format, such as Country or Adult Contemporary. Radio ads are typically either 60 or 30 seconds long, and the ads, like the medium itself, are felt as very personal to the listeners. According to a 2017 study conducted by iHeartMedia (which owns many radio stations), 86 percent of those surveyed agreed they "felt a deep connection with a favorite radio personality," while 61 percent said they had "considered or purchased a product recommended by their favorite radio personality."[4] One of the most effective forms of radio commercials has the station announcer read the ad copy aloud. Many think of this as one of the earliest forms of influencer marketing.

Digital audio pureplays continue to grow in importance, particularly with younger listeners. About one-fifth of the U.S. population listens to services such as Spotify or Pandora, while nearly half of all those aged 12–24 years say that they have listened to Spotify "in the past month."[5] When they do so, if they are not paying for an ad-free experience, they are exposed to ads that have been targeted precisely, similarly to digital ads.

## Print

As noted earlier, newspapers are the oldest media channel to include advertising, and were the reason behind the first ad agencies (who created and bought the ads). Magazines, too, are a centuries-old medium. For decades, both enjoyed strong consumer and advertiser support. Today, both struggle to sustain their businesses in terms of the number of printed copies they sell and the revenues they can generate from advertising. Newspapers in the U.S. have seen ad dollars drop in half in the past five years, and many have closed completely in both large and small markets. Outside the U.S. too, the news is not that much brighter. The only positive area is in digital subscriptions, which now account for half to two-thirds of all subscribers to major publications such as the *Times of London* or *Wall Street Journal*.[6] While readers of the printed newspaper had little personal connection to the journalists, the digital forms have encouraged far more interaction between writer and reader. Newspapers were traditionally considered influential in and of themselves, since they attracted a more educated and affluent population, but their digital forms may prove more powerful due to the two-way communications they allow.

Magazines were, from the start, considered an upscale and influential medium too. The first titles published aimed for a broad readership, which they achieved: About 60 percent of the population could be reached through *Life, Look,* and *The Saturday Evening Post.* Things changed with the arrival of television in the 1950s. In response to that powerful new medium, magazines became more specialized and focused, whether aiming at female homemakers (*Good Housekeeping, Woman's Day*) or car enthusiasts (*Car and Driver*) or those who smoked cigars (*Cigar Aficionado*). Separate titles were developed for specific agricultural groups (*Cotton Farmers, Western Livestock Journal*) and for businesses (*PC World, Oil and Gas Journal*). Readers either committed to buying issues every week or month or subscribed for a year at a time, providing the magazines—and their advertisers—with a loyal, dependable audience and reliable revenues. Once the Internet came along, people found they could get the same—or similar—content at no cost and subscriptions plummeted. Unlike newspapers, which set up paid gateways to their online content, magazines initially tried to maintain subscriptions by reducing their cost. This ended up putting many of them out of business, and many of today's titles are published less frequently, charging more for the digital access and testing higher-priced single-copy sales.

The role of influencers in traditional print was twofold. First, as noted earlier, readers of newspapers and magazines were considered inherently *influential* in that they were usually thought of as opinion leaders who would talk to others about what they had read (both content and advertising). Even today, when companies want to speak to a large audience with an important message, they often take out full-page ads in the newspaper. Examples include corporate mergers, public relations disasters, or reassurance at times of financial uncertainty.

### Outdoor

What used to be a highly local and quite manual industry, with people hired to paste posters onto boards (the original "billboard"), has become a much more digitally oriented and measurable ad medium. While advertisers do not invest huge sums in outdoor advertising, there has been steady growth in ad spend in recent years.

One of the biggest benefits that outdoor advertising offers is that the messages are delivered while people are outside of the home and, it is claimed, going to or going from stores. The digital component (billboards connected to the Internet, which allows for messages to be changed from a central location) enables outdoor messages to be immediately responsive to changes in the environment, such as highway billboards that change their message based on how busy the roadway is, or boards that encourage passers-by to engage in social media. For example, Kraft Jell-O created a "pudding face" on a billboard that smiled or frowned based on how people reacted to a Twitter post.

In terms of influencer marketing, outdoor advertising has not really played a large role to date. That has started to change, however, with the digital out-of-home component, as brands start to post influencer-created content on billboards, particularly at the local or regional level. When thinking of music and the creative use of outdoor, Spotify's global director explains "For us, [outdoor advertising] has become a social channel, and we trust that if the creative is compelling enough, people will do the work of amplification for us."[7]

## *Digital*

In the U.S., paid digital advertising spending is now larger than that of newspapers, magazines, and radio combined, and, by most calculations, even larger than the spend on television.[8] There are many forms of digital advertising. The most important ones are display (ad banners), video, search, and social. In many ways, the creation of these paved the way for influencer marketing to develop and grow. The first digital ads were static banners that put a brand's message in front of (if not in the way of) Internet users, allowing them to click through to the advertiser's website. As Internet speeds improved, brands started putting their TV commercials online, which over time developed into paid digital video ads created specifically for that platform. The notion of using the Internet to search for products and services created a huge shift in consumer behavior, replacing several other ways that people would look for information, including the Yellow Pages and classified advertising. Paid search was initially offered to advertisers by several digital companies, including (Microsoft) Bing and Yahoo; but today, according to eMarketer, Google is responsible for 61 percent of all search dollars.[9] Moreover, search advertising accounts for more than four in ten of all paid digital dollars.

Social media provides the foundation for influencer marketing; but, for advertisers, it is critical to all parts of the digital advertising ecosystem. Facebook, for example, is where the largest proportion of display ad dollars is spent.

## Owned Media

In some ways, owned media represent both the oldest and newest ways to influence consumers. As mentioned, some of the first radio and TV programs, for example, were "owned" or sponsored by popular brands. Yet, many categorize marketing influencers as fitting, at least in part, within owned media channels. Similarly, while products have appeared in (been "placed" in) TV shows and movies for at least 40 years, the development of brand websites has been noteworthy in the past 10 years.

All of these channels have grown, in part, due to advertisers' realization that paid media dollars alone were no longer sufficient to generate awareness or preference or sales. Moreover, the ability of marketers to measure the impact of their owned media has helped them expand their interest and investment in these areas. Here, ownership may be long term, as when a brand owns their website and has total control over all aspects of its presentation. Also, the ownership might be for a contractually bounded term and limited in control as found in brand placement and sponsorship.

### Product Placement

Once advertisers no longer had their name in front of a TV program, and as the clutter of traditional TV advertising increased, companies started looking for other ways to put their brands in front of people. Product or brand placement provided an easy way to do so, inserting a box of Kellogg's cereal in a sitcom, for example, or having people drink conspicuously from a cup of Pepsi on a reality show.[10] This practice originated on the big screen, with numerous films incorporating branded products or services into the scene (for a fee). That practice goes as far back as silent movies of the 1920s, but for later audiences, one of the most famous placements was that of the Hershey candy Reese's Pieces, which appeared in the film *E.T.* in 1979 and caused a tripling of the product's sales. The film franchise that is best known for product placement is that of *James Bond*, from Aston Martin luxury cars to Omega watches. Today, in the U.S., product placement is estimated to be worth about $12 billion.[11]

It should be noted that product placement is not considered legal in some countries. In the U.K., it was first permitted in 2011, and only in certain types of programs and for products that can be advertised on television (excluding alcohol or gambling, for example).[12] In many European countries where TV was at some point state owned and not dependent on advertising, product placement was thought of as "surreptitious advertising," possibly with the intention to mislead.[13] This is illustrated by rules in Austria, where product placement is forbidden in public broadcasting unless it comes within programming from elsewhere.[14]

This kind of promotion might be considered an indirect type of influencer marketing, since advertisers hope that when consumers see a TV or film star using their brand of mobile phone or drinking their beverage, those people will be influenced to buy those products.

## Sponsorship

The practice of companies paying an organization to put their name in front of an event is today a multibillion dollar global business. From seeing innumerable brand names on a NASCAR driver's car and clothing, to sports stadiums named for a brand, to having brand logos and products associated with a pop star's worldwide concert tour, sponsorship allows companies to own a piece of the event. Worldwide sponsorship spending reached $66 billion in 2019.[15] The vast majority of spending is consistently in sports (70 percent), followed by entertainment (10 percent) and causes (9 percent).[16] Deals within sponsorship oftentimes specify if athletes or entertainers will have a role in communicating about the sponsor and, in this way, employ influencers.

Importantly, sponsor investments are leveraged through sponsorship-linked marketing programs to support the deal that is set for 3, 5, or 25 years.[17] In fact, when leveraging ratios are 2:1, twice as much is being spent leveraging the deal in other ways. This often includes influencer marketing. Perhaps the most famous of these relationships is that of Nike's sponsorship of Michael Jordan and the subsequent development of the iconic Air Jordan shoe.

In many ways, there is a natural evolution from sponsorship to influencer marketing, partly because athletes can be thought of as some of the earliest influencers. People like Michael Jordan and Lionel Messi were paid by companies such as Nike and Adidas to be seen in public wearing those brands and talking about them whenever possible. Influencers have, however, reached a point of success that may invite brand managers to circumnavigate expensive team or event deals and go directly to the source of passion and emotion.

---

**MELDING SPONSORSHIP AND INFLUENCER MARKETING AT THE SUPER BOWL**

Anheuser-Busch became the official beer sponsor of the NFL Super Bowl in 1988. While everyone is familiar with their advertising, their overall Super Bowl activation has become an event sensation in its own right. For many years now, Anheuser-Busch (AB Inbev) have activated their relationship with the NFL and the Super Bowl through development of a Budweiser-themed hotel. For example, for the 2020 Super Bowl in Miami, they secured the hotel Nautilus by Arlo and turned it into the BudX Hotel.[18] The hotel interior was reimagined to match the Budweiser brand in color, style, and every detail down to the pillows. They also invited 200 influencers from 20 countries to support content creation. These "kings of culture" each had more than one million followers. They even created an on-site studio where these international influencers could work with professional producers and content editors to allow them to maximize real-time videos featuring the branded environment.[19] In addition to the BudX venue, there were curated events including concerts, a karaoke competition, and other brand-linked activities like a Gillette pop-up barbershop for influencers.[20] Their goal was to generate impressions through influencers, and it is estimated that they gained over a billion.[21]

## Earned Media

Some might believe that earned media did not exist before the rise of social media channels such as Facebook or Tencent. However, the notion of brands using media to earn their consumers' trust and respect is really not new at all. People have been talking about brands for as long as those products have existed! Admittedly, it has always been difficult for marketers to manage those conversations and ensure that the brand is always mentioned in a positive light, while the reality is that we often tell others about a product when we have had a negative experience with it. The management of brand stories developed into a full discipline, public relations, which began its growth about the same time as paid media did, in the early 20th century.

Today, brands rely much more on the digital conversations than those that occur in person and face to face. Thanks to social media platforms such as Facebook, Instagram, Twitter, or TikTok, every time a person likes a brand, shares content about it with their friends, sends a tweet, or pins it to their favorites, the marketer can not only count those measures but also monitor if those actions lead to a future sale. Because of the reliance of marketing influencers on social channels, many consider that they are under the earned media umbrella.

### Word of Mouth

Despite the fact that brands look to social media to earn consumers' appreciation, the reality is that nearly three-quarters of conversations about brands still happen face to face.[22] That is why many companies are interested in directing their ad messages to opinion leaders, hoping that if those people have a positive view about their brands, they will in turn talk to their friends and acquaintances and convince them to adopt the same affirmative opinions toward the brand. Offline influencers are estimated to represent about 10 percent of all consumers, but are much more likely to talk to friends and family about their opinions (and brands).[23] Some advertisers have taken a more active role in making this happen, hiring brand ambassadors who are paid to educate people about the brand and advocate for it. For example, college students on campus are hired to give away samples of Sephora makeup. Others are full-time positions that involve brand education and advocacy to customers or distributors. Yet others are employees trained to speak about the brand in a positive way no matter their role in the company.[24] This is analogous to influencers who are paid by marketers to promote a brand through social media.

Research has shown that what people say about brands in person can be very different from how they talk about the same brands online. In a 2017 study conducted by Engagement Labs, it was shown that social media brand conversations do not mirror the broader chatter happening beyond the social sphere. There was a minimal correlation between the two kinds of talk. Indeed, the research showed that those who talk about a brand online are typically a different group of people from those who mention brands offline. That leads to the finding that when marketers encourage online conversations about a brand, it is not likely to lead to offline discussion.[25]

## Social Media

As noted earlier, advertisers spend billions of dollars placing their brand messages overtly on social media platforms such as Facebook or Instagram or YouTube. But in doing so, they are also hoping to further encourage consumers to respond to the brand and its messages, thereby earning the advertiser support by boosting awareness, preference, or even sales. Social media became a global consumer and advertising phenomenon even before influencers. Advertisers have flocked to these platforms to reach their target audiences, which are in the millions, or sometimes billions of people. Instagram, for example, reports it has one billion monthly users worldwide, while YouTube attracts two billion. TikTok, one of the newer social platforms, has grown to 370 million users in the past year or two, with no signs of slowdown.[26] It is the popularity and power of social media that fueled the explosive growth of influencers in marketing.

According to a survey conducted among 2,094 people in the U.S. and the U.K. who follow influencers, nearly three-quarters (72 percent) of those confirmed that they were using social media more during the pandemic than previously, a figure that rose to 84 percent among Gen Z respondents. Perhaps not surprisingly, the type of content that people want to follow has shifted, with people now saying they are following influencers more in categories such as news and information, food, and physical well-being. In addition, those who follow influencers have shifted their opinion in the type of content that they are looking for from those content creators. At a time where people may be stuck at home or in quarantine, they are more eager to see how-to videos (40 percent said this), memes or humorous content (37 percent), or short-form videos (33 percent). The social media platforms used to follow influencers have not changed significantly due to Coronavirus Disease (COVID). That is, YouTube, Facebook, and Instagram are the top three cited by influencer followers.[27]

## Influencers in the Ecosystem

Estimates on how many influencers there are vary and change frequently. There is no single source of truth. What is being captured, however, is the amount being spent on this kind of marketing. The growth has been phenomenal. In the U.S., total spending is believed to have gone from $1.7 billion in 2016 to $8 billion in 2019, and expected to touch $15 billion by 2023.[28] It is estimated that marketers are currently putting about 10 percent of their budgets aside for influencer marketing, on average. Surveys suggest that that amount will increase in years to come.

A survey of marketers and agencies conducted in December 2019 found that 60 percent had run up to five campaigns in the prior year, while 15 percent deployed an "always-on" influencer strategy. Marketers are increasingly recognizing the benefit of using influencer content in other media channels. While the top two choices for where that content would go were paid social and the brand's organic social efforts, four in ten (41 percent) said they would incorporate it into the brand website.[29]

While the use of influencers is growing rapidly in the U.S., it is even more prevalent in Asia, particularly China. In one study, reported by Cision and PRWeek in November 2018, the proportion of marketers saying they felt confident in their ability to find the right influencer and impact consumer behavior was highest in China, where more than eight in ten (81 percent) agreed with that statement, compared to half that percentage (39 percent) of U.S. marketers.[30] In another 2018 survey by the World Federation of Advertisers, two-thirds of companies surveyed reported that they planned to increase their spend in influencer marketing in the next year.[31]

---

## A TRADE ASSOCIATION FOR INFLUENCERS

In 2020, the American Influencer Council Incorporated (AICI) was formed as a nonprofit trade organization.[32] It was created by influencers for influencers to support the integrity and growth of the influencer market in the U.S. Their mission has five prongs as summarized here.[33]

1. **Learning and Development** with the goal of providing intellectual capital to advance digital marketing education at the university level and offer mentoring support for the next generation of influencers;
2. **Consumer Transparency** with targeted lobbying of the Federal Trade Commission (FTC) to cooperatively adhere to, promote, and improve Endorsement Guidelines;
3. **Standardization and Professional Ethics** by developing market-relevant operating standards to support innovation and ethical conduct;
4. **Data Science and Influencer Economy** with the goal of fostering digital economy research and analysis and examining the contributions of career influencers to the U.S. Gross Domestic Product (GDP);
5. **Public Goodwill** developed by creating an innovation lab, providing industry-relevant public service announcements, and hosting events promoting the influencer trade.

In part, the goal of the organization is to gain recognition of influencers as small business owners and entrepreneurs.

---

The extent to which marketers are employing influencers does vary by sector, with categories such as retail, fashion, and beauty relying quite heavily on this type of promotional activity. Media and entertainment companies are rapidly increasing their investments, with ViacomCBS purchasing an independent influencer company called WhoSay in 2018.[34]

However, not all influencers are alike. One way to differentiate them is in the number of followers they attract. Those with the largest following are considered macro influencers, then come the micro influencers with small to moderate follower counts, and lastly, there are highly specialized or niche players, known as nano influencers. One benefit of influencer marketing is that even small brands can use it to gain a larger voice in the marketplace.

Boxed Water used a #ReTree campaign with YouTube personality Megan de Angelis to promote its eco-friendly water, giving it the kind of attention normally reserved for much larger brands such as Dasani or Aquafina.[35] Some larger brands see an advantage in developing a relationship with micro or nano influencers before they become too famous. However, it is hard for any brand, but especially larger ones, to rely solely on influencers with a small following because they will naturally have a more limited reach. The decision on which type of influencer to work with may vary by country. In Asia, for example, celebrities are used more because they are considered more powerful in their ability to influence consumers than, say, in the U.S. or Europe. Many brands use a combination of macro and micro influencers.

Another important distinction is the platform that influencers use. While Instagram remains the most popular, followed by Facebook and YouTube, there is an increased interest among influencers on newer or more niche platforms such as TikTok for short-form videos and Twitch for live streaming.

The amount that brands are spending with individual influencers for individual posts is still a matter of debate. It is believed that influencers are being paid hundreds or sometimes thousands of dollars for a post. Then there are well-known celebrities such as Kylie Jenner, who is believed to be the highest-paid influencer. With 147 million followers on Instagram, she commands over $1 million per post.[36]

## Grassroots Marketing

Small business or entrepreneurial use of influencers is largely off the radar due to the fact that much of it is unpaid. A small business might contact others on LinkedIn and ask for a repost from someone with a large following or a comment from someone on Facebook.[37] The other approach frequently employed is to provide samples in the hope of a good word. One coconut oil company gained 218 mentions from influencers in various formats after providing a sample box.[38] Nonetheless, grassroots employment of influencers is strategically identical to that of larger more expensive campaigns. Influencer marketing can help small brands gain a larger "voice." Small businesses may have the extra burden to be clever in order for a small campaign to rise above the clutter.

As this chapter shows, the marketing ecosystem is expansive, with many different ways for brands to reach their prospects and customers, in paid, owned, and earned media channels. It is also an ecosystem that is always evolving, with new technologies which change how or where people consume media. Those, in turn, create new opportunities for marketers to deliver their messages. Influencer marketing is one such development, enabling brands to connect to consumers in ways that continue to further the evolution of their marketing ecosystems.

## Discussion Questions

1. Can you think of some examples where a brand's traditional advertising campaign was more memorable than the influencer campaign? How about the reverse, where the influencer campaign for a brand was more memorable than the traditional advertising campaign?
2. From the influencer campaigns you can recall, try to determine what the brand's marketing and/or advertising objectives were.
3. Compare and contrast the effectiveness of a brand's influencer campaign compared to its television advertising.
4. How could a marketer use an influencer with a radio campaign?
5. How influential are print ads compared to influencers?
6. What is the impact for a brand of featuring an influencer in their digital campaign?
7. Have you seen any influencers featured in out of home (outdoor) advertising? Do you think it was effective?
8. Can you think of ways for brand influencers to be placed into TV shows or movies?
9. If you were recommending to a company to feature an influencer in their sponsorship of a sporting event, whom would you suggest and why? How about a sponsorship of a music festival?
10. Which influencers did you learn about through word of mouth? How important was that means of communication to you?
11. Do influencers require social media platforms to be successful? Why or why not?
12. If you were advising a travel marketer on how best to utilize influencers in their marketing, how would you do so? What would you recommend?
13. What brands can you recall that you learned about through influencer marketing? Did you then hear or see them in other media channels? If so, which ones? Conversely, which brands have you seen or heard in traditional media channels, and then seen promoted by an influencer? How do you compare the two experiences?
14. How could or should grassroots campaigns take full advantage of influencers in their efforts?

## Notes

1. https://go.forrester.com/blogs/09-12-16-defining_earned_owned_and_paid_media/
2. www.nielsen.com
3. Ibid.
4. iHeartMedia presentation, 2019.
5. iHeartMedia, ibid.
6. Newspaper financial reports and websites.
7. https://www.thefashionlaw.com/the-advertising-beauty-of-a-billboard-in-the-age-of-instagram/
8. Zenith Media Global Adspend Report, 2020.
9. eMarketer, March 2020.
10. Karrh, J. A. (1998). Brand placement: A review. *Journal of Current Issues & Research in Advertising, 20*(2), 31–49.
11. www.statista.com, February 2020.
12. www.bbc.co.uk, February 2011.
13. Schejter, A. M. (2004). *Product placement as an international practice: Moral, legal, regulatory and trade implications.* 32nd Research Conference on Communication, Information and Internet Policy, Arlington.
14. Ibid.
15. https://ministryofsport.com.au/global-sports-sponsorship-spend-to-reach-65-billion-in-2019/
16. www.sponsorship.com/IEG/files/f3/f3cfac41-2983-49be-8df6-3546345e27de.pdf
17. Cornwell, T. B., Weeks, C. S., & Roy, D. P. (2005). Sponsorship-linked marketing: Opening the black box. *Journal of Advertising, 34*(2), 21–42.
18. www.eventmarketer.com/article/influencer-marketing-budx-hotel-super-bowl/
19. Ibid.
20. www.adweek.com/brand-marketing/budweiser-brought-200-influencers-to-a-hotel-for-super-bowl-weekend/
21. Ibid.
22. Engagement Labs study, 2017.
23. Keller, E., Fay, B., & Dodd, M. (2019, February). The power of everyday influencers in driving business outcomes. *Admap.*
24. Gelb, B. D., & Rangarajan, D. (2014). Employee contributions to brand equity. *California Management Review, 56*(2), 95–112.
25. Engagement Labs Study. (2017). *5 myths about social influence.* Retrieved from www.engagementlabs.com
26. Retrieved from individual platform websites.
27. Global Web Index, The Age of Influence, July 2020.
28. www.businessinsider.com, December 2019.
29. Linquia: The State of Influencer Marketing 2020.
30. Williamson, D. A. (2019, March). Global influencer marketing 2019. *eMarketer.*
31. Ibid.
32. www.thebeautyinfluencers.com/2020/07/15/%E2%80%8Bthe-american-influencer-council-launches-on-the-10th-anniversary-of-social-media-day/
33. Ibid.

34. Im, K. (2019, November 19). Sharing is caring. *Adweek*, 41. Used with permission of Adweek. Copyright ©2020. All rights reserved.
35. *Netbase: The 2019 complete guide to influencer marketing*. Retrieved from www.netbase.com
36. www.influencermarketinghub.com, March 2020.
37. https://mention.com/en/blog/influencer-marketing-as-a-small-business-owner/
38. https://smallbiztrends.com/2016/08/what-is-influencer-marketing-small-business.html

## Further Reading

Baetzgen, A., & Tropp, J. (2013). "Owned media": Developing a theory from the buzzword. *Studies in Media and Communication, 1*(2), 1–10.

Belden, C. (2013). Paid, earned and owned media: Convergence in social media. *Journal of Digital & Social Media Marketing, 1*(3), 243–250.

Childers, C. C., Lemon, L. L., & Hoy, M. G. (2019). #Sponsored# ad: Agency perspective on influencer marketing campaigns. *Journal of Current Issues & Research in Advertising, 40*(3), 258–274.

Cornwell, T. B., & Kwon, Y. (2020). Sponsorship-linked marketing: Research surpluses and shortages. *Journal of the Academy of Marketing Science, 48*, 607–629.

Eagle, L., & Dahl, S. (2018). Product placement in old and new media: Examining the evidence for concern. *Journal of Business Ethics, 147*(3), 605–618.

Lovett, M. J., & Staelin, R. (2016). The role of paid, earned, and owned media in building entertainment brands: Reminding, informing, and enhancing enjoyment. *Marketing Science, 35*(1), 142–157.

Singh, S., & Sonnenburg, S. (2012). Brand performances in social media. *Journal of Interactive Marketing, 26*(4), 189–197.

# 3

# ENDORSERS AND INFLUENCERS CLARIFYING THE BOUNDARIES

With a basic understanding of the ecosystem within which influencer marketing sits, we now dig deeper into who influencers are. We start by exploring in greater depth the boundaries between endorsers and influencers, looking at the research that helps explain the differences. We then examine the key attributes of influencers and learn how influence spreads.

## Endorsers

The history of endorser research goes back decades and reviewing it can help us to understand how endorsing and influencing work. Perhaps the most influential work of all is that of Roobina Ohanian, who developed a scale to measure a celebrity endorser's perceived expertise, trustworthiness, and attractiveness.[1] These three attributes became the focus of future research and central to the understanding of the celebrity endorser's ability to influence purchase.[2] In fact, these three attributes were so central to how celebrity endorsers were selected, that other attributes were perhaps glossed over until found to be problematic. For example, music icon Rihanna was dropped from Nivea's personal care product endorsement advertising after it was decided that she was "too sexy" for the brand.[3]

## Matching

Another central part to understanding early celebrity endorser work is the match-up hypothesis.[4] Much of the research at this time was based on schema congruence where your past experience develops your

DOI: 10.4324/9781003037767-3

expectations within a specific context. For example, at a birthday party there is an expectation that there will be a cake and that candles will be blown out after people sing a celebration song. The idea was simple: When there is conceptual overlap between the endorser and the product or service that they endorse, communications are more effective.[5]

Subsequently called "fit" or "match," the advantage conferred on a good match between an endorser and product spawned a stream of research. When the match was only superficial, such as the phrase often seen in ads for pharmaceutical products that "I'm not a doctor but I play one on TV," expertise and trustworthiness were sacrificed for attractiveness, with questionable outcomes.

The match between the person and a celebrity also became an important consideration. For example, the congruence between the celebrity image and the ideal self-image impacts endorsement effectiveness.[6] Findings like this that highlight the role between the person and the persona they follow are important to influencer marketing because of the more direct relationship (real or perceived) on social media.

So, in essence, celebrity endorsers who match with the product and have the three attributes of trustworthiness, expertise, and attractiveness have been seen as the best endorsers. It has been shown to be important for an endorser to match with the product endorsed as well as with the person or consumer that is targeted in communications. What can be learned from the study of celebrity endorsers, spokespeople, and spokes-characters?

Here, we come to a point where the nature of content development plays a role in the trajectory from endorser thinking to influencer thinking. In the earlier times, an endorser was almost exclusively utilized in advertising that was controlled by the advertiser. This changed with the growth and development of the Internet. Social media enabled "the creation and exchange of user-generated content."[7] As influencers developed their own content, which may be influenced by a brand, the control has shifted from the brand to influencer. This notion of creating and sharing content that builds understanding of the person and their life gave rise to the concept of human brands.

## Human Brands

Before discussing human brands, it is useful to review the accepted definition of brand from the American Marketing Association. A brand is a name, term, design, symbol, or any other feature that identifies one seller's good or service as distinct from those of other sellers.[8] In terms of branding, here is where current trends and research in influencer marketing depart somewhat from established traditional thinking.

In 2006, Matthew Thomson described a "human brand" as "any well-known persona who is the subject of marketing communications efforts."[9] This idea is represented by an example Thomson provides of figure skater Michelle Kwan, quoted as saying: "When I go to the grocery store, people hug me. But that's OK. People do know me. They've seen me grow up on television."

The thinking in 2006 recognized the value of relatable, competent, and authentic human brand relationships but still viewed human brands as particularly effective endorsers, a partner for companies seeking positive associations. While the term "human brand" was coined, the perspective was still under the legacy of endorser thinking. We can now easily see human brands in various walks of life, which do not begin as celebrities, such as in sport.[10] It is a fact that human brands can arise without celebrity status.

We need yet another concept, that of "personal branding," to truly capture many modern influencers as self-made, personal brands. Self-branding involves individuals developing a distinctive public image for commercial gain and/or cultural capital.[11] Researchers from Canada analyzed the acclaimed athletes David Beckham and Ryan Griggs to point out how their on-and off-field brand building produced very different professional images and media personas.[12] David Beckham has a far-reaching personal brand and wealth that he has parlayed in areas such as Major League Soccer team joint ownership.[13] At this point, due in large part to individual ownership of content, we can apply the concepts of marketing and branding to a person.

---

## THE ACCIDENTAL INFLUENCER TEACHES OTHERS ABOUT PERSONAL BRANDING

Afshan Nasseri was attending university when a photo of her, dressed in Saudi Arabian pants and an Aeropostale brand top, jumpstarted her role as a South Asian-American influencer.[14] She grew her blog about her homeland and connected with a cultural community, worked with a skincare startup that utilized Indian ingredients, and then became a successful freelancer with her own mini agency.[15] She now teaches others how to develop their own personal brand and consults on strategy.

How does the human brand fit into our understanding of influencer marketing? Researchers keen to learn what aspects of humanness are associated with the concept of attachment in influencer marketing conducted two studies.[16] With Instagram as the context, they first asked people to name a social media influencer they follow and then asked: "Why do you like and follow this person on Instagram?" They found that influencer personas were associated with inspiration, enjoyability, visual aesthetics, similarity (to oneself), physical attractiveness, expertise, and authenticity. They found that informativeness, visual aesthetics, and expertise were associated with the social media influencer's content. In the second study, they examined how influencers, as human brands, fulfill needs that people have. They considered how influencers, when they are inspiring and present aesthetic content, provide ideal standards that others like and aspire to possess. By being in some ways similar and enjoyable, influencers provide a feeling of relatedness. When influencers provide informative content and expertise, they fulfill needs for experiencing competence. They found that each of these needs being fulfilled by the influencer then increases the level of attachment a person feels with an influencer. Finally, they found that attachment with the influencer is transferred to the influencer's endorsements, thus increasing the follower's willingness to buy products or services endorsed by the influencer. This process was only considered with human brands, and it is an open question if this would work with other personas such as animals, cartoons, or virtual influencers. What we have learned from research contrasting influencers and celebrities is that people identify more with influencers than celebrities, feel more similar to influencers than celebrities, and trust influencers more than celebrities.[17]

## Attributes of Influencers

Naturally, the individual traits of a person, or their projected characteristics as a persona, play a role in the relations they form both with the people being influenced and with brands, and in turn their responses to these relationships. Thus, the original three important attributes of attractiveness, expertise, and trustworthiness have been shown to apply equally well to influencers. In influencer marketing, other attributes come into play which, while possibly present in endorsements, are more profound now. Let's have a look at three attributes: popularity, contemporariness, and distinctiveness.

## Popularity

Celebrity endorsement depends on popularity; by definition, celebrities are well known. Endorsement also employs many everyday people who typically communicate based on their expertise. This might be a mom suggesting snacks for children, the roofer suggesting a solar panel brand, or the bass fishing enthusiast suggesting the best lure. These distinctions correspond roughly to mega/macro and micro/nano influencers. That said, popularity in terms of the number of followers is available as an indicator on most social media, and therefore is utilized in making assessments of influencers in a different way than in traditional endorsements.

- Mega influencers—over one million followers, typically celebrities, expensive;
- Macro influencers—100,000 to one million followers, typically content creators, expensive;
- Micro influencers—small following, typically viewed as authentic, affordable; and
- Nano influencers—very small, perhaps local and inexperienced following, affordable.

According to a survey of marketers and agencies conducted in December 2019, there was a clear interest in working more with micro influencers, cited by nearly eight in ten (77 percent) of the survey respondents.[18]

Research has shown that Instagram influencers with many followers are thought to be more likeable partly because they are more popular.[19] It is important that followership is central to influencer marketing, and this emphasis, while waning, does impact selection and strategy. Followership is found in some research to be less important than the engagement generated by the influencer.[20] The two, followership and engagement numbers, work together in delivering on marketer goals.

## NANO INTERIOR AND JUNGLE ENTHUSIASTS

It has been reported that 100 million copies of the *Bible* are printed each year but that twice as many IKEA catalogues are printed.[21] IKEA, the Swedish-origin, global furniture retailer, wanted to further fuel interest in their uniquely popular catalogue in Denmark. With this in mind, IKEA invited

390 female interior design enthusiast influencers aged 25–49 years to get their catalogue at a local IKEA store or have it shipped to them and then to take creative photos and post them.[22] The posts of the nano influencers encouraged thousands of others to buy a catalogue for interior redesign inspiration. IKEA has repeatedly utilized focused nano influencer campaigns for positive outcomes. Tribe Group worked with the retailer on their jungle collection showcasing the IKEA DJUNGELSKOG and URSKOG range of products.[23] In this case, nano influencers were invited to comment on the environmentally sustainable nature of the products and to feature jungle animals. Tribe Group reports 26 creator posts with a combined 304,402 followers resulted in an average of $.20 cost per exposure with 17,966 likes and comments.[24] As a plus, the conversations emphasized the importance of conservation and protecting wildlife, in particular, endangered species.

## Contemporariness

Influencers give brands the perception of being "with it." No better example of the allure of being cool can be found than in live streaming. Let's take a look at how influencers develop in this context.

Esports are electronic games played by professional teams in competitions, both online and offline. There are many genres such as fighting games, first-person shooters, real-time strategy, and multiplayer online battle arena games. Individuals often begin at a young age developing an online following through streaming their game play. One of the most popular streaming platforms for game players is Twitch.

The Twitch live-streaming platform hosts not only many activity categories such as gaming, but also music and performance, talk shows and podcasts, sport and fitness, science and technology, and even a category for just chatting. Importantly, across the platform, channel hosts are able to interact with their audience through a chat stream. Viewers and subscribers can post their comments, and the channel host might reply in real time. This interactivity, or even the potential for it, creates a community within the viewership, as well as a relationship with the channel host.

Take, for example, Jaryd Lazar, better known as summit1g. He was born in 1993, and developed a reputation in gaming via his competitive play in Counter-Strike: Global Offensive, a multiplayer first-person shooter game. He is a full-time professional gamer who receives income from audience donations, sponsorship, advertising, and branded merchandise such as T-shirts and mouse pads.

He utilizes social media to the fullest. For example, he posts his Facebook, Twitter, and YouTube links on Twitch. From Twitter, he posts his upcoming live sessions on Twitch as well as the game he will be playing. At the top of his Twitter page, he recognizes his partnerships with Monster energy drinks, Corsair gaming peripherals and hardware, Audio-Technica headphones, and CyberPower computers for gaming.

His persona is "adult rated" but that of a normal guy who likes to game. He might be chatting about vitamin gummies during play, but he may be doing so laced with profanity. During breaks his live audience, typically 70,000 to 100,000, sees an advertisement for the U.S. Armed Forces. His product giveaways on social media are clearly from him and his partners. His influence is subtle and believable. For those in the prime esports demographic of 18–34 years, he is a contemporary. He is an opinion leader, just as researchers have defined an influential person with a strong personal brand.[25]

## Distinctiveness

One way in which celebrity endorsers make communications more memorable is by supporting distinctiveness. The idea here is that certain aspects of an entity are notable, especially when there is something missing or different from the typical case.[26] Researchers tested this idea in an experiment by showing a shoe advertisement with a photo of an unknown endorser as a typical communication, and the exact same photo "cartoonized" as an out-of-the-ordinary communication.[27] Findings showed that the cartoonized advertisement was perceived as more creative (as new and divergent), which resulted in positive attitudes toward the advertisement and the brand, as well as increased purchase intention. Naturally, distinctiveness is context-specific. For example, cartoons would be the norm in advertising to children, so a cartoon ad would not stand out as different in that context.

Brand distinctiveness is different from brand differentiation, where a brand is set apart from others by some superior performance or unique benefits. Brand distinctiveness allows the brand to be picked out or brought into memory. Well-known examples include Mickey Mouse's ears, Tiger Woods, Nike, and the advertising style found in the Mastercard "Priceless" campaign.[28]

As yet another example, when Samsung launched their Note 7, they employed CyreneQ to document the phone's capabilities in 10-second videos that showed clips with her designer flair.[29] Her distinctive style is notable and consistent, offering a strong possibility of recall for the brand and connection of the capabilities of the phone to the brand.

The impact of the 2020 COVID-19 pandemic may have shifted the reasons people follow influencers as well as the traits that consumers appreciate most in the influencers they follow. A survey of 2,094 people who follow influencers, conducted in the U.K. and the U.S. in spring 2020, found revised preferences. The top three reasons for consumers to follow an influencer were to learn something new (51 percent), to be entertained or uplifted (49 percent), and to pass the time (49 percent). They had strong and clear expectations for brands that are in this space. The two main wishes cited in terms of what consumers want brands to do more of in the future are to be informative (noted by 47 percent of respondents) and to be a source of positivity (41 percent). At the other end of the spectrum, only 14 percent said they would want brands to do more to help improve their image or reputation. Such findings were deemed to be a result, in part, of the feeling that influencers' content during the COVID-19 pandemic offered a distraction and helped people feel more positive. Before the pandemic, the top three characteristics preferred in influencers were likeability, humor, and creativity; but during the pandemic, trustworthiness became the topmost sought-after quality. When people were probed more deeply to define what that meant, three-quarters of those responding said that passion for content, in-depth knowledge of a product or service, and transparency about the sponsorship were the most critical factors. In contrast, the number of followers or comments received was far less important.[30]

The question remains of how these various influencer attributes support a brand? In part, it is through the mental associations that are developed.

## Networks of Mental Associations

### Awareness and Recognition

One thing that a celebrity brings to a brand in endorsement is awareness, and in particular recognition. A person sees a familiar face and pays attention, and this is no less true for influencers than for traditional endorsers. Influencer marketing typically does not have the goal of building a memory for the relationship between the influencer and the brand, although this is possible. Rather, the goal is that the brand is recognized when found online or in a retail context. Sponsorship or partnership research, which has a longer history than influencer research, recognizes that for some brands, the sponsor's aim is an in-store change in behavior, when a brand seems appealing for some reason that is not consciously tied to the sponsorship.[31]

## Associations and Image

Another value in celebrity endorsers is their associations that are then shared with the brand. Thus, if a celebrity endorser has an image of success or coolness, such as George Clooney promoting Nespresso, this image could rub off on the endorsed brand. Awareness and image are the essence of brand knowledge.[32] They are how we come to know what a brand stands for, what it is used for, and what benefits it offers an individual.

## How Influence Spreads

Development of word-of-mouth advertising campaigns has been a mainstay of traditional advertising for decades. Strategies for "viral marketing" or "buzz marketing" employed influencers without celebrity status to communicate about products. Ford automobiles have been sold by giving cars to people, such as flight attendants, and simply asking them to drive around and hand out trinkets. Their early campaigns were explained this way: "We weren't looking for celebrities. We were looking for the assistants to celebrities, party planners, and disk jockeys—the people who really seem to influence what was cool."[33]

Brands' search for the essence of cool has not changed. What has changed is the ability of social media to leverage the noncelebrity voice. Approaches to accelerating communication about a product or service through influencers often take the form of product seeding, where people try a product, and message seeding, where influencers share a similar message.[34] The hope is that initiating product conversations from multiple starting points will result in cascades of influence.

## The Double Funnel

The overwhelming interest in influencer marketing regarding the sharing of content requires a different process funnel than is typically found in marketing as shown in Figure 3.1. This stems from the fact that there are two outcomes of immediate interest in influencer marketing. Brands are interested in sales or direct outcomes of social media influence for their brand, but they are equally interested in recommending behavior. In many marketing process models, their recommendation behaviors follow purchase and are dependent on the person's experience with the product. In influencer marketing, the ease of recommending without experience allows for interest in the influencer or the product to be communicated to others in an instant.

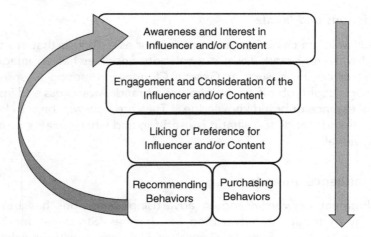

**FIGURE 3.1** The Double Funnel of Influencer Marketing

Another aspect of duality in influencer marketing stems from the fact that an individual exposed to the influencer's content may take interest in the influencer, the content, or both. Along each stage of the funnel shown in Figure 3.1, a person may become aware of and interested in the influencer and/or the content, and may then engage with or consider the influencer and/or content and like or prefer either or both. This duality can lead to recommendations (in terms of shares in particular) without purchase or, alternatively, purchase that may then also result in recommendation. In this sense, influencer marketing feeds its own funnel in a way that mass one-way traditional advertising rarely did.

## Cascades

The technical rise of influencer marketing must be in part associated with the possibility and attractiveness of online information cascades.[35] These occur when something such as information or an image is passed along. In social media, the interest is more technically on the number of new participants over time.[36] This is of interest to marketers who seek new customers. Work on cascades is, however, difficult to predict, and guidance from studying them suggests a strategy of having several starting points for a cascade. Interestingly, from a strategy perspective, researchers suggest that hiring an expensive influencer with a large following may be a more costly, and potentially less effective strategy, than hiring several ordinary influencers that hold an average or less than average influence.[37]

Adidas applied a multipronged approach to raise awareness of their Chinese women's volleyball team. They employed three main initiatives: supporting a team blog with professional photos of players that promoted each athlete as an influencer, creating and distributing six edgy videos of team play, and soliciting unique team chants for the team.[38] More than 5.5 million viewers watched the video.

In sum, there are many extensions from familiar celebrity endorsements that help us understand how influencer marketing works. That said, there are enough departures, twists and turns that as research on influencer marketing grows, it will expand our knowledge of the broader marketing and communication field.

## Discussion Questions

1. How important are the three attributes identified as important with endorsers (expertise, trustworthiness, and attractiveness) for influencer marketing? Can you think of some influencers who are particularly popular due to each one of these factors?
2. Consider some examples of influencers who were or are not good matches for the products they promote. Think about why the match does or does not work.
3. To which influencers do you feel most closely connected? What are the reasons for the connection? Which influencers do you feel least connected to? Again, why do you think that is?
4. Which category of influencer—mega, macro, micro, and nano— would work best for which brand? That is, name a brand for which each influencer category might work best.
5. How important is an influencer's popularity in your decision on whether or not to follow him or her?
6. Can you think of an influencer who is particularly contemporary or cool or one who is particularly distinctive? What is it about them that communicates these characteristics?
7. The idea of a double funnel, one that progresses an individual to purchase and/or recommend, suggests that influencers function differently from traditional media. How is this so?
8. Have you ever participated in a cascade? Were you aware of the huge popularity of the event at the time? What inspired you to share the content?

## Notes

1. Ohanian, R. (1990). Construction and validation of a scale to measure celebrity endorsers' perceived expertise, trustworthiness, and attractiveness. *Journal of Advertising, 19*(3), 39–52.
2. Ohanian, R. (1991). The impact of celebrity spokespersons' perceived image on intention to purchase. *Journal of Advertising Research, 31*(1), 46–54.
3. www.businessinsider.com/controversial-celebrity-endorsements-2012-8
4. Kamins, M. A. (1990). An investigation into the match-up hypothesis in celebrity advertising: When beauty may only be skin deep. *Journal of Advertising, 19*(1), 4–13.
5. Lynch, J., & Schuler, D. (1994). The matchup effect of spokesperson and product congruency: A schema theory interpretation. *Psychology and Marketing, 11*, 417–445.
6. Choi, S. M., & Rifon, N. J. (2012). It is a match: The impact of congruence between celebrity image and consumer ideal self on endorsement effectiveness. *Psychology & Marketing, 29*(9), 639–650.
7. Kaplan, A. M., & Haenlein, M. (2010). Users of the world, unite! The challenges and opportunities of social media. *Business Horizons, 53*(1), 59–68. Page 61.
8. www.ama.org/the-definition-of-marketing-what-is-marketing/
9. Thomson, M. (2006). Human brands: Investigating antecedents to consumers' strong attachments to celebrities. *Journal of Marketing, 70*(3), 104–119.
10. Carlson, B. D., & Donavan, D. T. (2013). Human brands in sport: Athlete brand personality and identification. *Journal of Sport Management, 27*(3), 193–206.
11. Khamis, S., Ang, L., & Welling, R. (2017). Self-branding, "micro-celebrity" and the rise of social media influencers. *Celebrity Studies, 8*(2), 191–208.
12. Parmentier, M. A., & Fischer, E. (2012). How athletes build their brands. *International Journal of Sport Management and Marketing, 11*(1/2), 106–124.
13. https://sports.yahoo.com/will-david-beckham-have-the-same-effect-on-mls-as-an-owner-that-he-did-as-a-player-224225849.html
14. www.deccanchronicle.com/in-focus/150720/saudi-arabian-pants-and-a-kinship-with-lucknow-afshans-journey-as.html
15. Ibid.
16. Chung-Wha, K., Cuevas, L. M., Chong, S. M., & Lim, H. (2020). Influencer marketing: Social media influencers as human brands attaching to followers and yielding positive marketing results by fulfilling needs. *Journal of Retailing and Consumer Services, 55*, 102–133.
17. Schouten, A. P., Janssen, L., & Verspaget, M. (2020). Celebrity vs. influencer endorsements in advertising: The role of identification, credibility, and product-endorser fit. *International Journal of Advertising, 39*(2), 258–281.
18. Linqua: The State of Influencer Marketing 2020.
19. De Veirman, M., Cauberghe, V., & Hudders, L. (2017). Marketing through Instagram influencers: The impact of number of followers and product divergence on brand attitude. *International Journal of Advertising, 36*(5), 798–828.

20. https://linqia.com/wp-content/uploads/2019/04/Linqia-State-of-Influencer-Marketing-2019-Report.pdf
21. https://brandheroes.com/blogs/case-studies/ikea-catalog-denmark
22. https://medium.com/@mnfst/8-brands-already-using-the-power-of-nano-influencers-fd4cdf8a6b8d
23. www.tribegroup.co/case-study/ikea
24. Ibid.
25. Li, F., & Du, C. T. (2011). Who is talking? An ontology-based opinion leader identification framework for word-of-mouth marketing in online social blogs. *Decision Support Systems, 51*(1), 190–197. https://doi.org/10.1016/j.dss.2010.12.007
26. McGuire, W. J. (1984). Search for the self: Going beyond self-esteem and the reactive self. In R. A. Zucker, J. Aronoff, & A. I. Rabin (Eds.), *Personality and the prediction of behavior.* (pp. 73–120). Orlando, FL: Academic Press.
27. Heiser, R. S., Sierra, J. J., & Torres, I. M. (2008). Creativity via cartoon spokespeople in print ads: Capitalizing on the distinctiveness effect. *Journal of Advertising, 37*(4), 75–84.
28. Romaniuk, J., Sharp, B., & Ehrenberg, A. (2007). Evidence concerning the importance of perceived brand differentiation. *Australasian Marketing Journal (AMJ), 15*(2), 42–54.
29. https://blog.hubspot.com/marketing/examples-of-influencer-marketing-campaigns
30. Global Web Index, The Age of Influence, June 2020.
31. Cornwell, T. B., & Humphreys, M. S. (2013). Memory for sponsorship relationships: A critical juncture in thinking. *Psychology & Marketing, 30*(5), 394–407.
32. Keller, K. L. (1993). Conceptualizing, measuring, and managing customer-based brand equity. *Journal of Marketing, 57*(1), 1–22.
33. Iacobucci, D., & Calder, B. J. (Eds.). (2002). *Kellogg on integrated marketing.* Hoboken, NJ: John Wiley & Sons. Strategies for Viral Marketing, Chapter 6, Maria Flores Letelier, Charles Spinosa, and Bobby J. Calder, page 91.
34. Haenlein, M., & Libai, B. (2017). Seeding, referral, and recommendation: Creating profitable word-of-mouth programs. *California Management Review, 59*(2), 68–91.
35. Bakshy, E., Hofman, J. M., Mason, W. A., & Watts, D. J. (2011, February). Everyone's an influencer: Quantifying influence on twitter. In *Proceedings of the fourth ACM international conference on Web search and data mining* (pp. 65–74). Hong Kong: ACM.
36. De Choudhury, M., Lin, Y. R., Sundaram, H., Candan, K. S., Xie, L., & Kelliher, A. (2010). How does the data sampling strategy impact the discovery of information diffusion in social media? *International AAAI Conference on Web and Social Media, Atlanta, Georgia, 10,* 34–41.
37. Bakshy, E., Hofman, J. M., Mason, W. A., & Watts, D. J. (2011, February). Everyone's an influencer: Quantifying influence on twitter. In *Proceedings of the fourth ACM international conference on Web search and data mining* (pp. 65–74). Hong Kong: ACM.
38. www.cision.com/us/2015/03/9-word-of-mouth-campaigns-that-rocked/

## Further Reading

Carrillat, F. A., & Ilicic, J. (2019). The celebrity capital life cycle: A framework for future research directions on celebrity endorsement. *Journal of Advertising, 48*(1), 61–71.

Hofmann, J., Schnittka, O., Johnen, M., & Kottemann, P. (2020). Talent or popularity: What drives market value and brand image for human brands? *Journal of Business Research*, forthcoming.

Torres, P., Augusto, M., & Matos, M. (2019). Antecedents and outcomes of digital influencer endorsement: An exploratory study. *Psychology & Marketing, 36*(12), 1267–1276.

Yoo, J. J. (2020). Does the model minority image work?: Consumer responses to the model minority stereotypes in ads. *Journal of Promotion Management*, 1–31.

# 4

# WHO ARE THE INFLUENCERS?

At first glance, there would seem to be nothing similar between Kylie Jenner and Christina Gabriele in the world of fashion and beauty, or Jamie Oliver and Laura Ramirez as food influencers. But in understanding the process that is happening between brand, consumer, and influencer at a deeper level, it becomes clear that those relationships are remarkably consistent in terms of key characteristics and potential outcomes. This chapter explores who influencers are from a conceptual level in order to better understand how they do what they do.

We start at a high level, looking at the broad characteristics of influencers. From this, we develop an Influencer Process Model that organizes both commonly addressed aspects of influencer marketing and evolving, new aspects. The key characteristics of influencers, influencer audiences, and brands are explored as are the main outcomes that each party gains from the process.

## Influencer Process Model

To help organize our knowledge of influencer marketing, Figure 4.1 presents a model of the influencer marketing process. The model introduces three stages: (1) formation of the influencer–influencee relationship via social bonding, (2) acquisition or development of a brand relationship, and (3) generation of outcomes of the tripartite relationship for each member.

In influencer marketing, there are three relationships of interest:

- between the person and the influencer,
- between the person and the brand, and
- between the brand and the influencer.

DOI: 10.4324/9781003037767-4

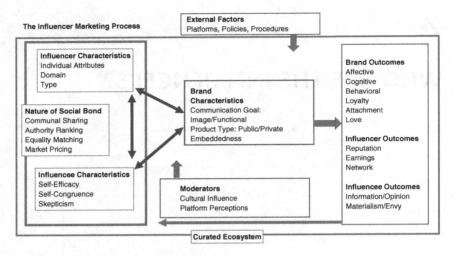

**The Influencer Marketing Process**

**External Factors**
Platforms, Policies, Procedures

**Influencer Characteristics**
Individual Attributes
Domain
Type

**Nature of Social Bond**
Communal Sharing
Authority Ranking
Equality Matching
Market Pricing

**Influencee Characteristics**
Self-Efficacy
Self-Congruence
Skepticism

**Brand Characteristics**
Communication Goal:
Image/Functional
Product Type: Public/Private
Embeddedness

**Moderators**
Cultural Influence
Platform Perceptions

**Brand Outcomes**
Affective
Cognitive
Behavioral
Loyalty
Attachment
Love

**Influencer Outcomes**
Reputation
Earnings
Network

**Influencee Outcomes**
Information/Opinion
Materialism/Envy

**Curated Ecosystem**

FIGURE 4.1 Influencer Process Model

These relationships are represented in Figure 4.1 with two-ended arrows between the relationship members. It is this tripartite structure that makes influencer marketing different from mass media marketing and more similar to sponsorship of sports, arts, and events. While a contract exists between the influencer and the brand, there is an independent relationship that the influencer holds with the person that, like the independent relationship a sports team holds with fans, means that the brand has less control over both the messages and the outcomes.

Figure 4.1 shows the Influencer Process Model ensconced in an ecosystem of curated relationships with others. Development of the influencer–influencee–brand relationship is influenced by moderators such as culture and platform perceptions. It is also affected by external factors such as social media platform policies and procedures. The development of the model starts with an examination of the characteristics of influencers and influencees and their social bonds.

## Characteristics of Influencers

For brand managers choosing influencers to represent their products and their values, there are two sets of characteristics to consider. The first regards the person and their individual attributes that make them a good influencer, while the second focuses on what makes that person a good influencer for *this* brand.

## Individual Attributes

In addition to the areas we discussed already in Chapter 3, such as trustworthiness, expertise, attractiveness, popularity, contemporariness, and distinctiveness, there are many positive personality traits to value in influencers. In most instances, a successful influencer is confident, even authoritative or passionate, and probably likeable to most. This is not to say that they may not share misgivings or mistakes, which can help make them relatable, but generally there is a tone of success.

In terms of working with any brand, it is helpful if influencers have a sense of the marketing role to be undertaken, perhaps a track record of experience showing that they are organized, know various platforms, and can offer the best content. It has been argued that irrespective of their size, influencers embody three marketing functions: access to an audience, an established endorser persona, and skills in social media management (as a strategist, producer, and community manager).[1] Paramount to almost any influencer selection is that the individual is engaging not only in their presentation but also in the audience response in terms of follows, likes, shares, and interactions. These counting measures important to the influencer marketing process are covered further in Chapter 7.

It has been noted that influencers with a high number of followers are viewed as more likeable and popular, but the reverse, not following others, can also negatively impact the influencer's likability.[2] There are many ways to consider the "followers/followees ratio" in terms of the impact it has on the perceiver. While individuals might accept that a celebrity with millions of followers could not possibly or thoughtfully respond in kind and follow back, with mid-level influencers, unwillingness to follow others or follow back may be interpreted as overly cold or self-important behavior. It is also possible to create the opinion that a high followers-to-followees profile might have been developed with paid or fake accounts, thus undermining perceptions of influence.

In addition to many "good to have" individual attributes that are true for almost any influencer and their relationship with both their own audience and the brand, there are two influencer characteristics that interact with the brand to determine the success of the relationship, namely influencer domain and type.

Audrey Schomer, in summarizing a research report from *Business Insider Intelligence* on influencer marketing, states that influencers can be categorized from the brand perspective as offering reach or niche. Reach influencers have followers, but Schomer writes, "As a general rule, targeted reach, cost-effectiveness, engagement, authenticity, and accessibility all go up as follower count goes down."[3] Because of their fame, mega and macro influencers may be viewed as somewhat general, with their defining niche simply being a household name. Therefore, one of the first strategic questions to ask, since it determines relevance for the brand, is: What is an influencer's domain of influence?

## Domain

Influencers can be categorized by the focus of their topical influence. That said, influencers can span domains and may drift from one to another. Having an identifiable domain of influence is important to brands because this supports trust in the influencer.[4] Following are some of the most popular and recognized domains.

- Arts
- Business/Technology
- Charity
- Entertainment/entertainers
- Fashion/beauty
- Food/beverage
- Health/wellness
- Home/family
- Music
- Photography
- Sport/fitness/athletes
- Travel/lifestyle.

While having a recognized area of knowledge or regular participation, expertise, or experience holds advantages, even micro- and nano-level influencers may be generalists of a sort. In recognition of this fact, Twitch has streamers that self-identify as having a "Just Chatting" channel where they discuss wide-ranging topics of interest. These are typically oriented to the demographic and psychographic profile of the influencer and the audience, such as high school students, college roommates, or vegetarians.

## Influencer Types

There are many ways to categorize influencer types.[5] They can include the following:

- Communication approach—blogging, vlogging, or posting comments or photos;
- Source of fame—reality TV star, athlete, journalist, photographer;

- Follower status—mega (celebrity), macro, micro, nano influencer;
- Motivation—financial, activist, politician, corporate, or nonprofit thought leader.

---

**FAME OF THRONES**

When the Home Box Office series Game of Thrones became popular so did the Icelandic actor, Hafþór Júlíus Björnsson, also known as "The Mountain." His fame in this role was utilized by the Israeli drinks company SodaStream to reach "sinks and dinks" (single income/double income no kids) demographics.[6] The "Join a Revolution" campaign played off a famous final season of Game of Thrones in communicating the company's unique culture. The campaign has had more than 50 million views and 100,000 shares.[7] Importantly, the actor was the key in departing from their long-standing demographic focus on families. The company could have focused instead on "mommy bloggers" but that would not have reached their new demographic of interest that had been revealed in marketing research.[8]

---

It must also be recognized that influencers change over time. In terms of their influence over others, they have been classified as (1) emerging influencers, (2) holding influencers, and (3) vanishing influencers.[9] While these categories may be useful, what the brand needs to understand is their style compatibility.

The influencers' approach to their domain, their content, and their style are discussed here as their influencer type. Researchers in Germany interviewed 15 German-speaking influencers. From these interviews, they identified four distinctive types of influencers based on their motivation as an influencer, content goal, and audience contact level: snoopers, informers, entertainers, and infotainers.[10]

- *Snoopers*, motivated by amusement and fun, discover social media platforms. They see content creation as a hobby, at least at first. They like to explore the technical side of content creation, are typically personally inspirational and encouraging, and regularly respond to their audience.
- *Informers* are content experts who are motivated to share their knowledge. They are responsible, trustworthy, and credible. They interact with followers via advice and suggestions related to their domain of knowledge.

- *Entertainers* focus on content that is amusing, enjoyable, and relaxing for their followers. They are motivated to offer their audience a good time. Entertainers "are often influence-entrepreneurs who have teams in the background supporting them in content creation and maintenance (e.g., cutting, filming, managing social media)."[11] Nonetheless, they are typically perceived as one entity, the one seen by the camera. Audience contact can be lower or impersonal based on the number of followers.
- *Infotainers* are a cross between informers and entertainers with a mix of motivations. While these are experts in a content domain, they may prioritize entertaining, personalized, and emotional content. Contact with followers may be limited or impersonal.

The orientation here is to consider influencer type as a communication style that must match with a brand. Put simply, fun brands need fun influencers, complex brands need informational content, and some brands need their serious or complex information to be made palatable.

Individual attributes, influencer domain, and style all come together to set the stage for what most argue is the most important ingredient for successful influencer marketing: authenticity. While authenticity begins here, it is the enactment of the influencer relationship that ultimately determines how authentic an influencer is. The role of authenticity is addressed in depth in Chapter 6.

## Influencee Characteristics

Clearly, the extent of influence possible in digital communication is in part related to the characteristics of the audience member. Some of these characteristics may be demographic. For example, adolescents have been shown to be more accepting of influencers having sponsorships and more compassionate than critical of influencers earning a living through sponsored content.[12] Beyond demographics and lifestyle or even psychographics that reflect an individual's values, attitudes, and opinions, what characteristics transcend the particulars of the person but are very influential in online social interactions?

That individuals vary in their susceptibility to advertising influence is not a new topic, but the extent to which it differs in influencer marketing may be.[13] At least three influencee characteristics impact bonds that are made with influencers and the sway they hold on outcomes. Each of these is discussed next.

## Self-Efficacy

Self-efficacy is people's belief in their ability to do things with the skills they possess.[14] Any course of action might come with some reflection on self-efficacy. For example, this is not a question of "do I *know* how to send a direct message in Twitter?" but rather "do I *believe* in my ability to communicate on the Twitter platform?" In other words, in this context, the question should be "do I believe in myself?"

Twitter self-efficacy was investigated as a characteristic important in how individuals respond to athlete influencers on the Twitter platform.[15] Twitter has a history of being difficult to use.[16] The researchers examining athlete endorsements on Twitter found that as a follower's Twitter self-efficacy increased, attitudes toward athlete endorsements on Twitter decreased. It appears followers admire an athlete endorser because of that athlete's ability to navigate a social media platform that they as followers have not been able to accomplish to their satisfaction yet. When one does gain self-efficacy on a platform, then perhaps those influencers don't seem as special. While it has not been investigated so far, influencers on platforms featuring short-form video, such as TikTok, may be impressive to others in part because they are successful with the short-form format, but this might wane as others gain belief in their ability to create content for this platform.

## Self-Congruence

Marketing has had a long-standing interest in the similarity of a brand's image to that of the potential consumer.[17] Someone might express this as "these shoes are so me!" In influencer marketing, self-congruence between a person and a product is important, but so is the self-congruence between the person and the influencer. Person–influencer congruence is often discussed in terms of the extent to which people are relatable, not distant and different. For example, the congruence between potential tourists and travel-oriented social media endorsers has been shown to contribute to intentions to visit a travel destination.[18]

Deciding that an influencer is similar to oneself naturally requires some assessment of the persona and some comparison to the self. This can be a worrisome undertaking. In explaining women's envy of social media influencers, a researcher found that the extent to which individuals compare themselves to others is influenced by having high self-consciousness and low self-esteem.[19] In short, identifying self-congruence with others is a natural tendency but can become problematic for some.

## Skepticism

The extent to which a person is suspicious of an influencer's motiva-tions affects his or her response to an influencer. Advertising skepticism, or the general tendency toward disbelief of advertising claims, varies across individuals.[20] Skepticism as a trait (a general tendency) originates, at least in part, from one's family experiences, but this is not a strong predictor of how skeptical one will be of advertising or other forms of promotion.[21] Nonetheless, it does vary from person to person, and the degree to which one is an advertising skeptic does influence the response to persuasion.

One important point in influencer marketing is the degree to which one can decide whether or not this is a marketing persuasion attempt. Importantly, one's skepticism is less likely to be activated when there is no little red flag saying, "they are trying to sell me something!" This flagging process depends on knowledge about the goals and tactics of a persuader.[22] How one reacts to persuasion attempts by social media influencers depends on both detecting them and also on one's own personal level of skepticism. This is one of the reasons that gov-ernments seek to protect their citizenry by requiring disclosures from influencers. If all influencer communications with sponsorship have the flag of #SponsoredAd, then people know if they want to be skeptical or not. Full disclosure might in fact be better than discovering a per-suasion attempt and reacting to this duplicity.

## Social Bonds Between Influencer and Influencee

Following an influencer may seem as simple as a click, but there are calculations people make regarding how we make social bonds. Psy-chological anthropologists Fiske and Haslam describe four relational models people have when developing bonds: authority ranking, com-munal sharing, equality matching, and market pricing.[23] These types of bonds are shown in Figure 4.1, summarized here, and applied to influencer marketing.

The quick click for a celebrity, a well-known journalist, or a political candidate is a simple bond in that we know they will likely not follow back. *Authority ranking* is where some have social power over others in a particular context. This is seen across social media platforms in the recognition of celebrity status. Being well-known comes with dif-ferent expectations about following back.

*Communal sharing* bonds are found when people feel that they have something important in common. They could start with the fam-ily, but sports, ideology groups, book clubs, or anything around which individuals form groups could become the basis for communal sharing. One can, for example, join established groups on the business networking site LinkedIn such as school and university alma mater, companies, and nonprofits. Formal and informal groupings are made by following individuals, groups, and organizations that share an interest. Joining a group where one feels membership is different from following a peer.

*Equality matching* is a relationship where people are keeping track of what others do or contribute, and is oriented toward having the right balance. This can be seen with micro and nano influencers, when the follower anticipates a follow back.

Lastly, *market pricing* bonds are found when social meaning is attributed to proportions of something that is valued. For example, influencers talk about their ratio of likes versus dislikes for a post. Here, having more likes than dislikes demonstrates the insight was "right" or at least in keeping with their followers' beliefs. People vote with their feet and influencers often preface controversial statements with "I may lose some followers, but. . . . " Followers have become social currency, which then becomes linked to monetary compensation for influencers, since their follower numbers indicate their attractiveness as an influencer. The market pricing model is inherently competitive since maximizing value is central.[24]

As the authors recognize, these four social bonds are found as composites, where a mix of social bonds is always at play. Regarding sport, a person might follow a journalist from ESPN with no expectation of a follow back (authority ranking) and may follow her college team just for updates (communal sharing); but when a game is on she expects responses and reposts from in-the-know local influencers (equal matching) and may stop following a local authority that is on the wrong side—as she and others see it—on a controversial play decision (market pricing).

## Brand Characteristics

Brands have many characteristics, but several aspects of a brand weigh heavily in what type of influencer relationship is best and how this relationship might unfold. Here we consider three characteristics of a brand that set the stage for how communications will be received: (1) the communications goal that often but not always stems from the nature of the product, (2) the product type in terms of its private or public use, and (3) the extent to which the brand is already embedded in a communications network with a history and expectations that have been built over time.

### Communications Goal: Image/Functional

Most practical guidelines for initiating a brand–influencer relationship begin with the idea that there must be some form of connection between the two. In essence, it must make sense to the person seeing a post that this influencer made it. The influencer's domain of interest and expertise, as well as his or her type or style of presentation, must match the brand's communication goals. Is the top priority to build associations for the brand as contemporary and cool or is it to demonstrate how the product solves a problem? This goal orientation should direct brands' search for influencers in their domain and with a style that works with their goals. However, it is a two-way process, and the influencer may offer his or her own ideas to the brand on how to accomplish the brand's goals.

When ticketing company SeatGeek wanted to push features of their app product via YouTube, they contacted influencer David Dobrik. Rather than detail aspects of the app as SeatGeek had wanted, Dobrik pitched the idea of surprising a friend with tickets to the World Series and shared this experience with followers.[25] This move from functional message to image story was successful and led to another 20 campaigns between the influencer and SeatGeek and garnered over 150 million views.[26]

According to Global Web Index's 2020 consumer survey, when people who follow influencers were asked what they value most in discovering brands via influencers rather than other channels, four in ten (40 percent) noted that it was the benefit of seeing the product in action, while one-third (35 percent) said it was finding products they would not have known about otherwise. The latter was the most important quality among younger, Gen Z consumers.[27]

### Product Type: Public/Private

Privately consumed products, like a mattress that people do not see, are very different in terms of marketing than public products, like an Apple watch, that would be highly visible to others. Public consumption comes with a degree of self-consciousness.[28] The degree to which a product is observed by others during consumption is important in influencer selection. For example, fashion, perhaps the epitome of public consumption, is best suited to an influencer who can wear clothing with style. While this seems obvious, even for technology products, social influence and adoption tendency are greater when an innovation is publicly consumed.[29] For privately consumed products, the facts matter, and an influencer who knows how to communicate them is best suited to these products.

## Embeddedness

The extent to which the consumers of a brand are already engaged with a brand and are embedded in a network of relationships surrounding it is important to how a person might react to any communication by an influencer. One way this becomes problematic is when a brand launches a campaign with paid influencers and ignores the organic influencers already in a community.[30] Professional sports teams, for example, have a community and a relationship with fans and sponsors, which is important when new actors or new messages are considered. This is analagous to the brand's history of advertising because people hold expectations about what the brand is and how it behaves.

Social embeddedness for an organization, or its brand, refers to the way it is connected to other actors in a web of social attachments.[31] A brand engaging an influencer in its already strong social media network should have marketplace advantages over a brand without a network. For example, Nutella, a chocolate and hazelnut sandwich spread, has an extensive, active brand community with an already strong link with consumers via interaction.[32] Any influencer who might be engaged to work with the Nutella brand would have to be accepted as genuine by the already established community. This functions similarly for a person having a long-time link to an influencer; new brand relationships need to be in keeping with expectations.

## Moderators

A host of factors could moderate the way the three-part relationship develops, including culture and platform perceptions. Figure 4.1 depicts an arrow influencing the relationship.

## Culture

Naturally, there are cultural sensitivities, and what works in one country may not work or even be allowed in another. There may be additional ways in which influencer relationships might be moderated by culture. Research on celebrity endorsers finds that the country of origin for both the branded product and the celebrity makes a difference in response to the relationship.[33] In considering brands marketed in China and India, one study found that a match between endorsers (actors Jackie Chan in China and Akshay Kumar in India, respectively) was not as important for a U.S. product (Fossil brand watches) as was the U.S. actor, Tom Cruise. However, this was not the case when individuals were ethnocentric, or held a negative bias against foreign-made brands. In that situation, a local celebrity improved evaluation of a foreign-made brand.

## Platform Perceptions

Another moderator of the tripartite relationship between influencer, audience, and brand is where the relationship unfolds. For example, the response to an influencer's post varies depending on his or her use of a blogging channel versus a Facebook post.[34] A blogger on his own channel may be regarded as an expert and could influence awareness through his expertise whereas on an entertainment-oriented, cluttered environment like Facebook, a well-known individual with a large following and a style in keeping with the platform may be more successful.

## Outcomes for the Brand

The varied outcomes that a brand desires from its influencer campaign include liking or preference (affect), awareness of the brand or understanding of its image or use, and trial or purchase of the brand (behavior). Influencer marketing should also be able to develop loyalty or regular purchase, or even attachment to the brand or brand love. Brand attachment occurs when there is a bond developed with the product that involves one's self-image.[35] Brand love results in having a passion for the brand, wanting to use it and not be without it, and holding positive feelings of connection and confidence in the brand.[36]

## Outcomes for the Influencer

Successful influencer outcomes beget more influencer opportunities. If effective, influencers build reputations and grow their network, while simultaneously generating incomes. Influencers are often paid for the posted content, for reactions to their content, or both. For example, in a survey of 400 influencers, a mid-level influencer (with 10,000 to 100,000 followers) reported charging between $250 and $400 for a blog post accompanied by online sharing.[37] These blog posts may be available for years, so this helps not only to bring income to the influencer, but also to develop a reputation over time.

Influence is in part determined by the identification with an influencer. For example, individuals identifying with athletes, and wanting to be like them, can lead to positive team-related intentions as well as a sense of community with other fans.[38] Influencers also can lose followers if they communicate about brands. A research conducted on

Instagram found that as celebrity influencers post brand-related content, followers drop off, but then shortly after, follower numbers improve, likely through the addition of new followers.[39] Clearly, repeated brand-oriented posts would eventually reduce the celebrity's following and thereby damage their brand equity—those values the influencer has in perceptions of their followers.

## Outcomes for the Influencee

Outcomes for followers can be positive or negative. There is a value in the communications offered by influencers, but given the discussed tendencies for self-comparisons in social media, there can be negative outcomes for sensitive groups. We consider both sides of the argument.

### Information/Opinion

Advertising or marketing communications of all kinds are argued to have an economic value by informing potential consumers of offerings in the marketplace. There is also a value in learning about new topics of interest. Fashion-interested followers on Instagram value originality and uniqueness in the opinion leaders that they follow.[40] Moreover, if the followers feel that the opinion leader fits with their own personalities, this strengthens the tendency to follow the fashion leader's advice.[41] Gaining information and valued opinions can give consumers a feeling of "being in the know."

### Immersion/Experience

Going to a music festival like Coachella or attending an event like the Super Bowl would be an enjoyable experience. Research has shown that interacting via social media while attending events furthers one's feeling of immersion in the experience and alters one's perception of time (speeding it up).[42] While this research did not specifically consider event-related interactions as arising from being a follower of a musician or athlete, outside the laboratory, interaction with content is often spurred by influencer posts. In short, content creation during an event or activity can improve experience through deepening the feeling of immersion.

### Materialism/Envy

There may also be a negative outcome for followers. Researchers have found, for example, that among teens in Singapore, imitation of media celebrities and perceptions of peer influence predict materialistic consumption values.[43]

Research conducted in South Korea explored the extent to which upward social comparison to influencers produces feelings of envy.[44] In a longitudinal study of females, "those who frequently see influencers' social media and those who are interested in postings about the daily life of influencers (but not informational postings) were more likely to compare their lives to those of influencers."[45] This in turn led to feelings of envy one month later.

## Curated Ecosystems

The existence and influence of echo chambers, where opinions are amplified and not challenged by alternative views since they are not included in the group, has become a concern in politics as social media evolved as a major source of information. Echo chambers have been observed in policy debates[46] and to some degree in sports.[47] That they can influence exposure to ideas is well established, but more research is needed to understand the extent to which they profoundly influence behavior.[48]

While the more sinister-seeming echo chamber is perhaps not as relevant to marketing as to politics, it is the case that, through their interactions, individuals and influencers develop what we could call a "curated ecosystem" (shown in Figure 4.1 as bounding the influencer marketing process). It is put forward here to describe the natural tendency to develop a digital ecosystem of similar others with similar opinions and views.

We have a natural tendency toward others who are like us and thus toward their influence (this is called social correlation). We also have an environmental pull where proximity (e.g., location, membership) brings individuals into the same circles.[49] So, we tend to associate online with similar others as well as those close to us. Several research examples of these tendencies have been found, such as where Twitter users and their followers have been shown to share opinions.[50] In terms of geographical closeness, Foursquare found that those with social relations likely do check-ins at the same locations.[51]

Although they can be observed, we do not yet know the influence of curated ecosystems on consumer behavior, but one would expect that they limit the entry of novel ideas and reinforce similarity. That individuals, through their own decisions, and through recommendation algorithms (that offer them more of the same based on their search and interaction histories), should surround themselves with the familiar and agreeable should not be surprising. Nonetheless, it does create a barrier to entry when the curated ecosystem is relatively closed and an advantage to those inside in terms of the likelihood that their views and any recommendations will be amplified.

## External Factors

The various social media platforms, or channels where influencer marketing is undertaken, set many aspects of the policies and processes the influencer must follow. In addition to the guidance and control of social media platforms, there are other pressures on influencer behavior. Influencer marketing platforms such as Upfluence, AspireIQ, #paid, CreatorIQ, and Tagger designed to support the discovery of influencers also seek to organize and monitor their behavior.[52] In order to be considered for some of the discovery platforms, influencers have to behave in particular ways that are valued by the platform. Further, as we discuss in Chapter 5, governmental oversight is expected to be a more profound external influence over time.

## Discussion Questions

1. Think of some influencers who have successfully spanned several domains. How have they done so? Are there any influencers you can think of who have been less successful in crossing areas of expertise?
2. Using the four influencer types that researchers in Germany developed (snoopers, informers, entertainers, and infotainers), consider who you would put into each category. Are there other types you might define?
3. In making the decision on whether or not to follow (or keep following) an influencer, which of these three influence characteristics was most significant: self-efficacy, self-congruence, and skepticism?
4. Imagine you were advising an athletic shoe brand on which influencer they should consider to achieve their communication goals. These goals could be related to image, or they could be functional. Whom would you recommend for each goal, and why?
5. Think of brands like Nutella, where the brand is already deeply embedded within its user community. Now think of the influencers they do—or could—work with, and why that relationship might be improved.
6. Consider the platforms on which you find influencers, such as Twitter or Instagram. Now think about how, or whether, that particular platform makes a difference in how you perceive the influencer. How might the influencer act differently if their content appeared on a different platform?
7. Consider the outcomes of influencer marketing on the brand, the influencer, and the influencee. Which one is most important, and why?

8. Think of a time where you followed an influencer because you knew others who already did so. Why did you continue to follow them? Or why did you stop doing so? How important do you think the echo chamber effect was on those decisions?

## Notes

1. Campbell, C., & Farrell, J. R. (2020). More than meets the eye: The functional components underlying influencer marketing. *Business Horizons, 63,* 469–479.
2. De Veirman, M., Cauberghe, V., & Hudders, L. (2017). Marketing through Instagram influencers: The impact of number of followers and product divergence on brand attitude. *International Journal of Advertising, 36*(5), 798–828.
3. Schomer, A. (2019). Influencer marketing 2019: Why brands can't get enough of an $8 billion ecosystem driven by Kardashians, moms, and tweens. *Business Insider.* Retrieved from www.businessinsider.com/the-2019-influencer-marketing-report-2019-7
4. Liu, S., Jiang, C., Lin, Z., Ding, Y., Duan, R., & Xu, Z. (2015). Identifying effective influencers based on trust for electronic word-of-mouth marketing: A domain-aware approach. *Information Sciences, 306,* 34–52.
5. https://grin.co/blog/types-of-social-media-influencers/
6. www.cmo.com.au/article/633195/sodastream-reveals-why-disruptive-influencer-campaigns-vital-reaching-new-audiences/
7. Ibid.
8. www.travelmindset.com/20-influencer-marketing-examples/
9. Liu, S., Jiang, C., Lin, Z., Ding, Y., Duan, R., & Xu, Z. (2015). Identifying effective influencers based on trust for electronic word-of-mouth marketing: A domain-aware approach. *Information Sciences, 306,* 34–52.
10. Gross, J., & Wangenheim, F. V. (2018). The big four of influencer marketing: A typology of influencers. *Marketing Review St. Gallen, 2,* 30–38.
11. Ibid.
12. van Dam, S., & van Reijmersdal, E. (2019). Insights in adolescents' advertising literacy, perceptions and responses regarding sponsored influencer videos and disclosures. *Cyberpsychology: Journal of Psychosocial Research on Cyberspace, 13*(2).
13. Barr, T. F., & Kellaris, J. J. (2000). Susceptibility to advertising: An individual difference with implications for the processing of persuasive messages. In *North American Advances* (pp. 230–234). Provo, Utah: Association for Consumer Research.
14. Bandura, A. (1986). The explanatory and predictive scope of self-efficacy theory. *Journal of Social and Clinical Psychology, 4*(3), 359–373.
15. Cunningham, N., & Bright, L. F. (2012). The Tweet is in your court: Measuring attitude towards athlete endorsements in social media. *International Journal of Integrated Marketing Communications, 4*(2).
16. www.chicagotribune.com/lifestyles/ct-social-media-twitter-for-beginners-20160202-story.html

17. Dolich, I. J. (1969). Congruence relationships between self-images and product brands. *Journal of Marketing Research, 6*(1), 80–84.
18. Xu, X., & Pratt, S. (2018). Social media influencers as endorsers to promote travel destinations: An application of self-congruence theory to the Chinese Generation Y. *Journal of Travel & Tourism Marketing, 35*(7), 958–972.
19. Chae, J. (2018). Explaining females' envy toward social media influencers. *Media Psychology, 21*(2), 246–262.
20. Obermiller, C., & Spangenberg, E. R. (1998). Development of a scale to measure consumer skepticism toward advertising. *Journal of Consumer Psychology, 7*(2), 159–186.
21. Obermiller, C., & Spangenberg, E. R. (2000). On the origin and distinctness of skepticism toward advertising. *Marketing Letters, 11*(4), 311–322.
22. Friestad, M., & Wright, P. (1994). The persuasion knowledge model: How people cope with persuasion attempts. *Journal of Consumer Research, 21*(1), 1–31.
23. Fiske, A. P., & Haslam, N. (2005). The four basic social bonds: Structures for coordinating interaction. In M. W. Baldwin (Ed.), *Interpersonal cognition,* (pp. 267–298). New York: Guilford Press.
24. Blois, K., & Ryan, A. (2012). Interpreting the nature of business to business exchanges through the use of Fiske's relational models theory. *Marketing Theory, 12*(4), 351–367.
25. https://digiday.com/marketing/treat-like-real-media-channel-brands-changing-work-influencers/
26. Ibid.
27. Global Web Index, The Age of Influence, 2020.
28. Fenigstein, A., Scheier, M. F., & Buss, A. H. (1975). Public and private self-consciousness: Assessment and theory. *Journal of Consulting and Clinical Psychology, 43*(4), 522.
29. Kulviwat, S., Bruner, G. C., II, & Al-Shuridah, O. (2009). The role of social influence on adoption of high-tech innovations: The moderating effect of public/private consumption. *Journal of Business Research, 62*(7), 706–712.
30. www.deconstructoroffun.com/blog/2019/2/26/10-mistakes-to-avoid-in-influencer-marketing
31. Uzzi, B., & Gillespie, J. J. (2002). Knowledge spillover in corporate financing networks: Embeddedness and the firm's debt performance. *Strategic Management Journal, 23*(7), 595–618.
32. Gabrielli, V., & Baghi, I. (2016). Online brand community within the integrated marketing communication system: When chocolate becomes seductive like a person. *Journal of Marketing Communications, 22*(4), 385–402.
33. Roy, S., Guha, A., Biswas, A., & Grewal, D. (2019). Celebrity endorsements in emerging markets: Align endorsers with brands or with consumers? *Journal of International Business Studies, 50*(3), 295–317.
34. Hughes, C., Swaminathan, V., & Brooks, G. (2019). Driving brand engagement through online social influencers: An empirical investigation of sponsored blogging campaigns. *Journal of Marketing, 83*(5), 78–96.
35. Whan Park, C., MacInnis, D. J., Priester, J., Eisingerich, A. B., & Iacobucci, D. (2010). Brand attachment and brand attitude strength: Conceptual and

empirical differentiation of two critical brand equity drivers. *Journal of Marketing, 74*(6), 1–17.

36. Batra, R., Ahuvia, A., & Bagozzi, R. P. (2012). Brand love. *Journal of Marketing, 76*(2), 1–16.
37. www.socialmediatoday.com/news/what-i-learned-from-surveying-over-400-influencers/564612/
38. Carlson, B. D., & Donavan, D. T. (2017). Be like mike: The role of social identification in athlete endorsements. *Sport Marketing Quarterly, 26*(3).
39. Guyt, J. (2018, June 1). *Celebrity equity on Instagram.* presentation at the European Marketing Association Conference, University of Strathclyde, Glasgow, UK.
40. Casaló, L. V., Flavián, C., & Ibáñez-Sánchez, S. (2020). Influencers on Instagram: Antecedents and consequences of opinion leadership. *Journal of Business Research, 117*, 510–519.
41. Ibid.
42. Tonietto, G. N., & Barasch, A. (2020). Generating content increases enjoyment by immersing consumers and accelerating perceived time. *Journal of Marketing.* doi:0022242920944388.
43. La Ferle, C., & Chan, K. (2008). Determinants for materialism among adolescents in Singapore. *Young Consumers, 9*(3), 201–214.
44. Chae, J. (2018). Explaining females' envy toward social media influencers. *Media Psychology, 21*(2), 246–262.
45. Ibid.
46. Goldie, D., Linick, M., Jabbar, H., & Lubienski, C. (2014). Using bibliometric and social media analyses to explore the "echo chamber" hypothesis. *Educational Policy, 28*(2), 281–305.
47. Frederick, E., Pegoraro, A., & Burch, L. (2016). Echo or organic: Framing the 2014 Sochi Games. *Online Information Review, 40*(6), 798–813.
48. Dubois, E., & Blank, G. (2018). The echo chamber is overstated: The moderating effect of political interest and diverse media. *Information, Communication & Society, 21*(5), 729–745.
49. Tang, J., Chang, Y., & Liu, H. (2014). Mining social media with social theories: A survey. *ACM Sigkdd Explorations Newsletter, 15*(2), 20–29.
50. Weng, J., Lim, E.-P., Jiang, J., & He, Q. (2010). Twitterrank: Finding topic-sensitive influential twitterers. In *WSDM* (pp. 261–270). New York City, New York.
51. Ye, M., Liu, X., & Lee, W. C. (2012, August). Exploring social influence for recommendation: A generative model approach. In *Proceedings of the 35th international ACM SIGIR conference on research and development in information retrieval* (pp. 671–680). Portland, Oregon: ACM.
52. https://influencermarketinghub.com/top-influencer-marketing-platforms/

## Further Reading

Bessi, A. (2016). Personality traits and echo chambers on Facebook. *Computers in Human Behavior, 65*, 319–324.
Cunningham, N., & Bright, L. F. (2012). The tweet is in your court: Measuring attitude towards athlete endorsements in social media. *International Journal of Integrated Marketing Communications, 4*(2), 73–87.

Derdenger, T. P., Li, H., & Srinivasan, K. (2018). Firms' strategic leverage of unplanned exposure and planned advertising: An analysis in the context of celebrity endorsements. *Journal of Marketing Research, 55*(1), 14–34.

Dumont, G. (2017). The labor of reputation building: Creating, developing and managing individual reputation. *Consumption Markets & Culture,* 1–17.

Krämer, N. C., & Winter, S. (2008). Impression management 2.0: The relationship of self-esteem, extraversion, self-efficacy, and self-presentation within social networking sites. *Journal of Media Psychology, 20*(3), 106–116.

# 5

# HOW INFLUENCERS ARE REGULATED

When U.S. retailer Lord & Taylor paid 50 fashion influencers in 2015 up to $4,000 each to post a photo of themselves wearing a flowing, paisley dress from the company's Design Lab collection, they did not require the bloggers to say in the post that it was an ad. That was found to be in violation of the Federal Trade Commission Act of 1914. The FTC, whose mission is to protect consumers and promote competition, ensures that companies do not engage in unfair or deceptive marketing.[1]

This chapter considers the regulations that are in place today for influencers, at federal, state, and local levels in the U.S. Comparisons with regulations in other countries around the world are made. Following this, we look at the implications for public policy.

As with many aspects of influencer marketing, regulation is still evolving. Legal and regulatory matters rely on precedent and prior rulings, so changes typically happen slowly as new cases are brought to the courts or other regulatory bodies. The landmark First Amendment ruling on free speech, Brandenburg vs. Ohio (1969), which used a "clear and present danger" standard, had in fact first been applied in Schenck vs. United States back in 1919. In the Brandenburg case, the state of Ohio had found Clarence Brandenburg guilty of inciting violence at a Ku Klux Klan rally. The Supreme Court overturned the decision, citing Brandenburg's First Amendment right to free speech.[2] This ruling appeared to overturn the 1919 decision the Court had reached, in Schenck vs. United States, when Charles Schenck's distribution of flyers during World War I advocating resistance to the draft were not protected by the First Amendment because they represented

DOI: 10.4324/9781003037767-5

a "clear and present danger" in and of themselves.[3] This is just one example of why legislation on influencers has been happening fairly slowly and has been implemented primarily as extensions of law or guidelines created years earlier.

Because influencers are, in most instances, promoting brands, companies, or ideas, it is actually quite easy to monitor them under the broad auspices of each country's advertising regulations. The devil lies in the details, however. Should influencers be regulated as endorsers? Are their posts covered by rules similar to those of print ads or social media?

According to the International Council for Advertising Self-Regulation (ICAS), 17 of the 24 countries it monitors had implemented or were developing guidelines for influencer marketing as of January 2020. There are three main areas of regulation: disclosure, compensation, and fraud. Each is covered here.

## Disclosure

The primary consideration for regulation of individuals as influencers is that they need to clearly disclose their relationship with the brands they help promote. As the FTC's *Disclosures 101 for Social Media Influencers* notes, "If you endorse a product through social media, your endorsement message should make it obvious when you have a relationship ('material connection') with the brand."

The term "material connection" includes a financial one if the brand is either giving the influencer products or paying them to promote the items. This is in line with the FTC's mandate that all ads should be *honest* and *truthful*. It is the responsibility of the influencer to provide the proper disclosures to the public. To make a disclosure "clear and conspicuous," advertisers should use plain and unambiguous language and make the disclosure stand out. Consumers should be able to notice the disclosure easily. They should not have to look for it. So, it should not be buried among hashtags or require the viewer to click somewhere else. If the endorsement is displayed through an image or a video, the disclosure needs to be placed on those items.[4]

There is no specific wording mandated for disclosures in the U.S. However, the same general principle—that people get the information they need to evaluate sponsored statements—applies across the board, regardless of the advertising medium. The guidelines are, however, quite prescriptive. In general, disclosures should be:

- close to the claims to which they relate;
- in a font that is easy to read;

- in a shade that stands out against the background;
- for video ads, on the screen long enough to be noticed, read, and understood; and
- for audio disclosures, read at a cadence that is easy for consumers to follow and in words consumers understand.

A key consideration is how users view the screen when using a particular platform. For example, on a photo platform, users paging through their streams will likely look at the eye-catching images. Therefore, a disclosure placed above a photo may not attract their attention. Similarly, a disclosure in the lower corner of a video could be too easy for users to overlook. Moreover, the disclosure should use a simple-to-read font with a contrasting background that makes it stand out. It should also be a worded in a way that's understandable to the ordinary reader. Ambiguous phrases are likely to be confusing. For example, simply flagging that a post contains paid content might not be sufficient if the post mentions multiple brands and not all of the mentioned brands were paid.

The big-picture point here is that the ultimate responsibility for clearly disclosing a material connection rests with the influencer and the brand—not the platform. This is indeed the stance taken by major social network platforms. Facebook explicitly notes on its website that publishers and influencers remain responsible for understanding their legal obligations to indicate the commercial nature of content they post. For most influencers today, the easiest way to stay within regulatory requirements is to include "#Ad" or "#Sponsored" prominently and clearly in their posts.

Marketers have a responsibility here too. They need to vet potential influencers to ensure that they are not already connected to competing or inappropriate brands. Both influencers and marketers should be trained to understand the law in this area, and influencers should be monitored to make sure they are complying with the rules.[5]

Failure to comply does bring consequences. The FTC cracked down on entertainment giant Warner Brothers, which used influencers on YouTube to promote one of its games, without identifying that it had paid them to do so. Under the terms of the settlement, Warner Brothers was banned for failing to disclose similar deals in the future and it cannot pretend that sponsored videos and articles are actually the work of independent producers. Whether the FTC takes action on influencers does depend on the overall impression of the content posted, including whether consumers take "likes" to be material in a potential consumer's decision to patronize a business or buy a product.[6]

Disclosure is a common theme in the global regulation of influencers. In the United Kingdom, the regulation falls under the purview of the Advertising Standards Authority (ASA). Its Committee of Advertising Practice (CAP) Code states that all ads "must be obviously identifiable as such." Similarly, Australia's Advertising Code of Ethics states that all advertising must be "clearly distinguishable," a standard repeated in many other countries.

In Russia, what constitutes influencer marketing is addressed on a case-by-case basis by the Federal Anti-monopoly Service (FAS).[7] Disclaimers have no specific wording or required position in messages but should be clear to consumers regarding the content being advertising.[8]

In the Netherlands, the key criterion is deciding if there is a *relevant relationship* between a brand and an influencer. Where that exists, the content distributor (influencer) is responsible for transparently disclosing the relationship.[9]

Perhaps one of the most interesting countries in terms of their approach to influencer marketing is China. The Chinese market has over 800 million active Internet users with an e-commerce marketplace estimated as $1.8 trillion in 2022.[10] The majority of consumers there (68 percent) report that they are influenced by social media when making a digital purchase (compared, for example, to 76 percent in India and 41 percent in Italy).[11] It has been argued that influencer marketing in China is well ahead of other countries in terms of integration (or blurring of the lines) of influencer and commerce with e-commerce conducted directly from the social media app. This may be due to China's influencer incubators (as backed by online retailer Alibaba and electronics giant Lenovo) where new key opinion leaders (KOLs) are nurtured.[12] One of these incubators, Ruhnn Holdings, has been listed on the NASDAQ stock exchange.[13] In contrast to the incubator agencies, small unions overseen by an individual manager are legally unprotected groups that support individuals, typically early in their career.[14] In fact, the number of KOLs in China has grown to the point that the ecosystem has a name, the Wanghong (Internet Celebrity) Economy.[15] Against this unique background, Facebook, Google, Twitter, YouTube, and other international social media platforms are banned.[16] Instead one finds streaming service Bilibili, microblog service Sina Weibo, messaging applications Tencent and WeChat, video channels Tuduo and Youku, as well as the short-form video channel, TikTok (Douyin).[17] Law in China requires that all influencer advertising content must be clearly identified, celebrities and influencers should be users of the product, and further have documentation to prove that they have first-hand experience with the product.[18]

Several countries' regulatory bodies have created step-by-step guides to help influencers ensure they are following the rules. In the United Kingdom, "Influencers' Guide to Making Clear That Ads Are Ads" offers a very consumer-friendly and easily read overview of the rules for influencers, answering questions such as "what counts as an ad?" and "how do I make it clear that ads are ads?" In addition, it includes an infographic for influencers (see Figure 5.1).

One influencer who came under scrutiny in the U.K. was Olivia Buckland, star of season 2 of *Love Island*. In October 2019, the ASA announced that a video that she had posted on Instagram in May 2018, where she applied eye shadow from the W7 Life's A Peach eye color palette—and essentially talked about how great it was—failed to be "obviously identifiable as a marketing communication."[19]

The other regulatory organization in Britain, the Competition and Markets Authority (CMA), expects influencers to disclose when they've received any form of monetary payment, a loan of a product or service, any incentive and/or commission, or product gift that they are posting about for free. As noted, their Code of Practice states that ads "must be obviously identifiable as such." For example, influencers Louise Thompson and Millie Mackintosh from the program "Made In Chelsea" were told to be more clear about the fact they were being paid to promote a watch and bottle of J20 whisky, respectively.

The hashtags #Ad and #Sponsored have become the unofficial standards for influencer disclosures. The influencer is responsible for adding this disclosure to communications. The only time that influencers do not need to make a disclosure is if there is no direct or paid relationship with the brand, and they talk about a brand that they simply like.[20]

Rules on influencer marketing are still evolving. In France, influencers are governed by the Digital Advertising and Marketing Communications Code, which covers 16 forms of digital marketing, from Advergames to Viral marketing, but has no language specific to influencers. Switzerland's influencers are covered by broad regulations that affect advertising. This means that, similar to traditional advertising, any such communication cannot be surreptitious and must be clearly separated from the content in which it appears. Influencers, therefore, are obligated to disclose their relationship to any sponsor. The Swiss self-regulation body, the Swiss Commission on Fairness in Advertising (SLK), announced its first decisions on influencer marketing in 2019. Where Switzerland differs, however, is that there are no clear rules yet on a standard way to label influencer communications. While there are strict labels required for television or radio ads, for instance, the same is not yet true for social media or influencer marketing.[21]

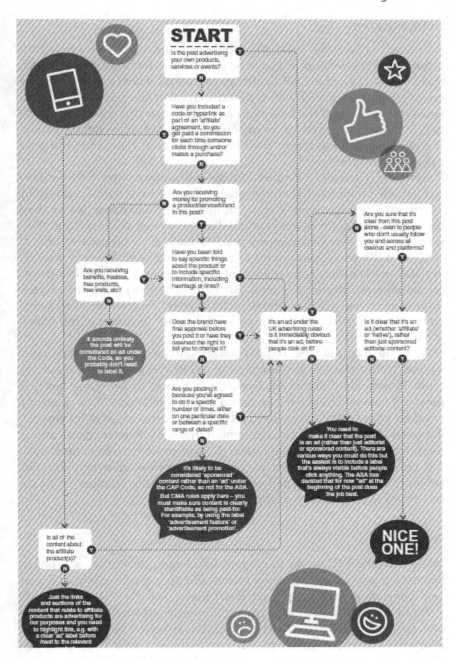

**FIGURE 5.1** Infographic: Is My Post an Ad?

*Source:* www.asa.org.uk/resource/influencers-guide.html

## Compensation

As noted earlier, the need for regulations around influencers often require that the influencer has received compensation from the advertiser. In the U.K., the CAP Code specifies that if there is any kind of commercial relationship with a brand that must be disclosed. That is, while it is not illegal for brands to pay people to promote their products in blogs, vlogs, tweets, or online articles, consumers need to know the endorsement has been "paid for." If this is not clear, then the post risks breaking the law.[22]

Similarly, Canada's Competition Bureau enforces the Competition Act, which prohibits misleading advertising and deceptive marketing practices. These provisions apply to influencer marketing just as they do to any other form of marketing. Influencers must disclose "that they were paid or otherwise compensated to feature" a product or brand.

One of the earliest examples of successful compensation for including user-generated customer content in advertising is Apple's campaign for its iPhone. Starting in June 2015, the company solicited photos from its customers. Those whose pictures were selected received some compensation, and had their photo licensed for inclusion in the #ShotoniPhone campaign ads.[23]

In some markets, the regulations around compensation are connected to the disclosure requirements. In Belgium and New Zealand, there is a twofold standard. First, there needs to be some kind of payment involved between the brand and the influencer. This does not need to be monetary; free products may be considered a "payment" if there is an expectation or requirement that the influencer posts about them. Second, the advertiser needs to have some type of control over the content, which may be as narrow as reviewing everything the influencer posts, or as broad as requiring a specific number of posts or vetting where and when the posts appear.

## Fraud

In the U.S., the FTC works to prevent fraudulent, deceptive, and unfair business practices in the marketplace and to provide information to help consumers spot, stop, and avoid them.

Problems with fraud can occur in a number of ways. A brand may pay an influencer or give them products at no or reduced cost for which the influencer agrees to promote them. But what happens if the influencer does not live up to that commitment? Many brands are wary of taking legal action, which would alert the public to the problem. Snapchat actually took such an action against an influencer, Luka

Sabbat, in 2018 after he did not create the Instagram stories and post for which he had been paid $60,000.[24] Today, most brands insist on a full legal contract with each influencer in order to lay out penalties if either side does not deliver on the contractual terms.

The practice of paying influencers who promote fraudulent or ineffective brands is another challenge facing the industry. The most visible example of this type of fraud was the 2017 Fyre Festival, where influencers and celebrities were paid to promote this music festival, which then imploded and failed terribly, resulting in bankruptcy for the organizers and lawsuits filed by would-be attendees. The organizer of the event, Billy McFarland, invited supermodels and Instagram influencers, such as Kendall Jenner, Bella Hadid, and Hailey Baldwin, to an island in the Bahamas to help promote "the music festival of the decade." But the promotional video was made before any of the actual plans had been finalized, and none of the influencers confirmed whether the information they promoted was in fact true, even though they had been paid to promote it. That is, the accommodations were never finished, and the island infrastructure was not ready for the thousands of people McFarland intended to show up. In fact, the promotions were so successful that nearly all the tickets were sold within 48 hours after going on sale. Even then, McFarland had far outspent the money he was taking in, leading to a shell game of securing some funds in order to pay down the larger amounts that he owed to others. He ignored all efforts to cancel even though it was clear to everyone else that it was going to be a complete disaster. That is indeed what happened, with people being asked to sleep in federal emergency management tents and eat sandwiches out of polystyrene containers. It took several days for the attendees to leave the island.[25] The fallout from the event, besides the legal actions that ensued, was the damage to consumers' trust in influencers, because those individuals had not noted that they had been paid and the information they shared with their followers was not completely true.

Other concerns include influencers that have fake impressions or followers or inflated (and false) engagement levels. Unfortunately, these problems are not always easy to identify, though more companies and technology are working to solve this, including the platforms themselves. One way for marketers to determine whether the followers are genuine is to examine the reported reach and engagement metrics. If the reach seems too high, it could be the influencer is paying to make his or her audience larger than it really is. Similarly, engagement rates can be manipulated to be higher than they really are for example, through using bots, or by buying impressions to artificially inflate the numbers. Software is being developed now to monitor this kind of fraudulent activity, in addition to the platforms themselves trying to clamp down.

Yet another area of concern is the extent of genuine interaction that an influencer can generate for a brand. However, an advertiser buying fake "likes" is very different from an advertiser offering incentives for "likes" from actual consumers. If "likes" are from nonexistent people or people who have no experience using the product or service, they are clearly deceptive, and both the purchaser and the seller of the fake "likes" could face enforcement action.

The *New York Times* ran an experiment to assess fake followers by setting up a fake Twitter account and paying a U.S. company to buy followers. They looked at the names and information of the followers gathered, and realized that most were fraudulent, with account names that were obviously fake and names that were simply a random collection of letters and numbers.[26]

One beauty blogger on YouTube created a video that discussed the problems within the beauty influencer community, including hints of collusion, blackmail, and extortion. Several YouTube celebrities have posted videos about their depression and unhappiness. However, when some of them talked about a mental health app called BetterHelp, which connects the user with mental health professionals, people reacted negatively, particularly because the app was found to be problematic. The YouTube promoters were felt to be making money from their, and other people's, problems. This insincerity is one type of fraud that is growing in the influencer space.

Another challenge is the growth of social media bots to fraudulently enhance the size of an influencer's followers. "Good" bots help in discovery of content or the simple promotion of a hashtag or key word. "Bad" bots are typically pre-programmed fake accounts that manipulate opinions and can be used to enhance an influencer's following. Bad bots constitute 24 percent of website traffic and good bots 13 percent, while human interactions account for the remaining 63 percent of traffic.[27] As an example, a company called Devnumi was found to have sold Twitter followers to people who then used the inflated numbers to sell their "influence" to brands.[28] Companies are now surfacing to look for this kind of fraud, and brands are increasingly putting clauses in their contracts with influencers that require confirmation on the number of followers.

In the U.S., the FTC has taken few actions against fraudulent influencer activity. They have mostly sent out warning letters. But in 2019, the Securities and Exchange Commission (SEC) settled a case they had brought against Floyd Mayweather, Jr., and DJ Khaled, who had been promoting investments in Initial Coin Offerings without mentioning they had been paid to do so. As noted in a *New York Magazine* article, "What may be awaiting the influencer-marketing industry is a 'Cambridge Analytica moment,' a form of fraud so calamitous that industry groups and tech platforms are shamed into adopting more drastic measures to police bad behavior."[29]

Concerns over fraud are driving some marketers to consider moving to micro influencers. They feel that the customer relationship may feel more genuine and trustworthy, there may be less risk of fraud, and investment costs will be much lower than paying well-known celebrities for every post. These micro influencers, despite having a smaller following, tend to create their own content on topics (or brands) that they use personally. The interest in this kind of influencer does vary by country; it seems more appealing to marketers in the U.S., Canada, Germany, and the U.K., and less popular in Asia. Brands that work with micro influencers include Benefit Cosmetics, Stella Artois, and Moët & Chandon, although all continue to work with celebrity influencers where it makes sense.

Marketers have turned to nano influencers with even smaller followings of under 5,000. While the numbers are lower, the cost for marketers also is lower. In addition, these people are thought to come across to others as more genuine and passionate about the brands they promote. There may not even be money involved as nano influencers may receive free products instead.[30]

Other marketers have shifted the very definition of influencers, enlisting help from their own employees. Rent the Runway created its own ambassador network of 5,000 people who are passionate about the service to encourage them to post online their positive feelings. Clorox created a panel of influencers, again relying in part on enthusiastic buyers of its products.[31] Macy's formed its Style Crew program, with more than 300 people (employees and customers) recruited to promote the store on their individual social media platforms. While those individuals are not receiving payments, they do get commission on any sales that they generate.[32]

While marketers look to various solutions to overcome the challenges of fraud, the problem remains significant. In July 2019, Professor Roberto Cavazos of the University of Baltimore estimated that advertisers would lose $1.3 billion that year due to influencer fraud, representing an average of 15 percent waste on money spent on influencers.[33]

Part of the problem is that the governmental authorities, such as the ASA in the U.K. or the FTC in the U.S., either have not been highly active in cracking down on bad players or have not publicized their actions. The former did publish, in January 2019, a list of 16 influencers who, it said, would improve their disclosures; the latter was forced to reveal (via a Freedom of Information request) that it contacted 23 influencers between November 2018 and July 2019 to warn them to clean up their act.

## Consumer Response to Regulated Messaging

Researchers from Belgium studied consumer response to the use of sponsorship disclosure on Instagram. They considered four types of messages: (1) those without a disclosure of any kind, (2) those declaring that they were not sponsored by the use of the #notsponsored hashtag, (2) those declaring material compensation (*I could try these for free and share my opinion*) with the #sponsored hashtag, and (4) those declaring financial compensation (*I was paid to try these and share my opinion*) with the #sponsored hashtag. The general finding was that disclosing content as having been sponsored increased a person's awareness of the communication as being an advertisement. This in turn resulted in more skepticism as well as negative brand attitudes. They also found that the message without a sponsor-related hashtag had no hashtag at all and therefore may not have garnered as much attention. Interestingly, the work also found that inclusion of the #notsponsored hashtag produced more positive brand responses because the communication was seen as not being promotional and therefore not drawing skepticism.[34]

---

## DISCLOSURE DEMANDS UNRAVEL INFLUENCER

Simone Anderson became an influencer after documenting her loss of over 200 pounds (92 kg).[35] With hundreds of thousands of followers, she became a glamourous fashion influencer. The 29-year-old from Auckland, New Zealand, is the subject of four complaints made to the ASA because two of her posts did not clearly communicate that she was being paid by brands for the content shared.[36] Both the posts were reviewed by a board of nine industry experts and were found to have issues with truthful presentation and failure to identify the posts as advertising.[37] Yet another complaint detailed how Anderson was selling gifted clothes online and claiming to donate the money received to charity; following the new complaint, she made the page where the clothes were being sold unsearchable.[38]

In another study of 232 U.S. university students, researchers asked about several behaviors and attitudes including the extent of the students' influencer-following behavior, attitudes toward sponsorship disclaimers, satisfaction with a favorite influencer, and purchase and recommendation behaviors. Interestingly, while attitudes toward disclaimers deterred the students' recommendation of an influencer-recommended product to others, it enhanced their own purchase. In fact, the extent of influencer following and participant attitude toward sponsorship disclaimers profoundly influenced their decision to purchase an influencer-recommended product.[39] This makes sense, in that the sponsored nature of the content makes clear it is an advertisement, and it is perhaps less appealing to share an ad. On the other hand, the truthfulness supports purchase.

## Implications for Public Policy

The social media platforms used by influencers have slowly started to step up their actions to protect consumers. For example, Facebook has stated it will do more to stop branded content for vaping, weapons, or tobacco, as well as pay greater scrutiny to content for alcohol or dietary supplements.[40] At the same time, recent work has shown that social media influencers hired by tobacco companies have garnered billions of exposures.[41]

One of the biggest challenges when it comes to the regulation of influencers is that, while the practice is global, the regulations are not. Brands that work with influencers must conform to the nascent regulations that are in place in each country in which they operate, and while the rules regarding influencers are becoming more aligned and alike, they are not (as this chapter has shown) uniform or final.

### INFLUENCERS AND TOBACCO

"A two-year investigation by the Campaign for Tobacco-Free Kids and Netnografica LLC, suggests that tobacco companies have been secretly paying celebrities to discretely but effectively advertise cigarettes on social media."[42] Findings posted online and registered with the U.S. FTC disclose that young social media influencers have been paid by tobacco companies to advertise their products. These campaigns are subtle, sometimes only showing the product in the context, not in use. Nonetheless, visuals support a positive image of smoking and of the brands. These campaigns violate the social media platform regulations forbidding the paid advertising of tobacco products. Further, the campaigns violate the industry's own commitment not to target young consumers. The investigation names Philip Morris International, British American Tobacco, Japan Tobacco International, and Imperial Brands as companies documented to have had more than 100 tobacco-promoting social media campaigns. These campaigns have been documented in reaching countries that specifically ban tobacco advertising.

It is also difficult to understand for both the brand and the influencer which rules and regulations in a country might apply to an aspect of their planned partnership. For example, copyright laws oftentimes not designed to apply to social media may be applied. Intellectual property developed by a social media influencer might be subsequently used in brand marketing outside the original social media post, and likewise a social media post developed with a brand might be used in some other way by the influencer.

Some might want to create a global regulatory framework for influencer marketing, but without a worldwide body to create or push for that, it seems unlikely to occur in the near term. Even in the broader world of advertising and marketing, the World Federation of Advertisers, a global nonprofit organization that represents the needs of marketers, does not have a position on the regulation of influencers. In contrast, academic researchers have recently called out the lack of research examining influencer marketing.[43] They note influencer marketing functions as largely unregulated and that as a new form of advertising, there is a pressing need for new research.

## Discussion Questions

1. Select posts from five different influencers and see how well they follow the U.S. guidelines on disclosures. Are there other guidelines you think should be included on how influencers disclose their brand relationship?
2. Should influencers be required to use the hashtags #ad or #sponsorship?
3. Does the knowledge that influencers have been paid by a brand affect how you respond to their posts? Why, or why not?
4. What safeguards might a brand put in place to help them avoid a situation such as similar to what unfolded with the Fyre Festival?
5. In choosing whether or not to follow an influencer, how important is it to you to know how many others already follow that individual?

6. Should there be more regulation to prevent fraud in influencer marketing? If so, what rules should be implemented? If not, why?
7. Imagine a hair care brand that has been working closely with a celebrity influencer. The influencer has been facing negative publicity for statements made online. How would you advise the brand to consider working with a micro or nano influencer? Who might you recommend to them?
8. Does seeing or knowing that an influencer is paid by the brand she promotes make you less likely to consider using the brand?
9. How effective do you find posts by employees? Are those more or less impactful for you than a paid influencer's posts? Are there other differences to consider?
10. Should there be more rules in place when influencers work with brands that promote potentially dangerous or unhealthy products?

## Notes

1. Owens, S. (2019, January 19). Is it time to regulate marketing influencers? *New York Magazine.*
2. 395 U.S. 444 (*more*).
   89 S. Ct. 1827; 23 L. Ed. 2d 430; 1969 U.S. LEXIS 1367; 48 Ohio Op. 2d 320.
3. 249 U.S. 47 (*more*).
   63 L. Ed. 470; 1919 U.S. LEXIS 2223; 17 Ohio L. Rep. 26; 17 Ohio L. Rep. 149.
4. Federal Trade Commission Disclosures 101 for Social Media Influencers.
5. Howell, J., Goodrich, M., & Beane, A. (2019, January 21). Influencers and the law. *Advertising Age*, 30.
6. Owens, S. (2019, January 17). *Is it time to regulate social media influencers?* Retrieved from www.nymag.com/intelligencer
7. https://talkinginfluence.com/2020/05/18/influencer-regulation-different-markets/
8. Ibid.
9. *International council for Ad self-regulation.* Retrieved from https://icas.global/advertising-self-regulation/influencer-guidelines/
10. www.forbes.com/sites/forbescommunicationscouncil/2020/01/07/what-we-can-learn-from-the-chinese-influencer-ecosystem/#78c6619d7e1e
11. www.chandlernguyen.com/blog/2019/03/02/china-influencer-marketing-what-you-need-to-know/
12. www.luxurysociety.com/en/articles/2019/06/the-future-of-influencer-marketing-is-in-china/
13. www.lexology.com/library/detail.aspx?g=e22d27c0-75ab-4515-963d-928fceb88371
14. Ibid.
15. https://matchmade.tv/blog/what-you-need-to-know-about-influencer-marketing-in-china/
16. www.investopedia.com/articles/investing/042915/why-facebook-banned-china.asp

17. Ibid.
18. https://talkinginfluence.com/2020/05/18/influencer-regulation-different-markets/
19. www.cosmopolitan.com/uk/entertainment/a23284419/alex-bowen-olivia-buckland-love-island-couple-married/
20. Disclosures 101.
21. Fehr-Bosshard, D., & Germann, L. (2019, December 5). Separation of advertising in #influencer marketing in Switzerland. *Vischer*. Retrieved from https://www.vischer.com/en/knowledge/blog/separation-of-advertising-in-influencer-marketing-in-switzerland-38577/
22. ASA.
23. Pullen, J. P. (2018, January). The highs and lows of influencer marketing and user-generated content. *ANA Magazine*.
24. Mumbrella, Insincere Influencers: How to handle ghosts, DVM Law Team.
25. "FYRE: The Greatest Party That Never Happened," Netflix (2018); "Fyre Fraud," Hulu (2018).
26. *How to ensure authenticity in influencer marketing.* 2020. Retrieved from www.influencerintelligence.com
27. www.imperva.com/blog/bad-bot-report-2020-bad-bots-strike-back/
28. www.nytimes.com/interactive/2018/01/27/technology/social-media-bots.html
29. Owens, S. (2019, January 17). *Is it time to regulate social media influencers?* Retrieved from www.nymag.com/intelligencer
30. Maheshwari, S. (2018, November 12). The newest influencers don't need big numbers. *New York Times*, B1.
31. Williamson, D. A. (2020, March). Influencer marketing and the path to purchase. *eMarketer*.
32. How to ensure authenticity in influencer marketing. 2020. Retrieved from www.influencerintelligence.com
33. Cavazos, R., as reported at www.cnbc.com/2019/07/24/fake-followers-in-influencer-marketing-will-cost-1point3-billion-in-2019.html
34. De Veirman, M., & Hudders, L. (2020). Disclosing sponsored Instagram posts: The role of material connection with the brand and message-sidedness when disclosing covert advertising. *International Journal of Advertising, 39*(1), 94–130.
35. www.dailymail.co.uk/news/article-8477717/Glamorous-influencer-reprimanded-failing-reveal-posts-sponsored.html
36. Ibid.
37. www.nzherald.co.nz/nz/news/article.cfm?c_id=1&objectid=12344561
38. Ibid.
39. Cornwell, T. B., Katz, H., & Pappu, R. (2019). *Influencer marketing: The role of self-efficacy and disclaimers.* Unpublished working paper, University of Oregon.
40. Hutchinson, A. (2019, December 18). Facebook expands brand collabs manager to include Instagram creators. *Social Media Today*.
41. Wexler, B. (2018, August 27). New investigation exposes how tobacco companies market cigarettes on social media in the U.S. and around the world. *Campaign for Tobacco-Free Kids*. Retrieved from www.tobaccofreekids.org/press-releases/2018_08_27_ftc

42. www.vapingpost.com/2018/08/30/big-tobacco-accused-of-paying-influencers-to-advertise-cigarettes/
43. Kees, J., & Andrews, J. C. (2019). Research issues and needs at the intersection of advertising and public policy. *Journal of Advertising, 48*(1), 126–135.

## Further Reading

Craig, D., & Cunningham, S. (2017). Toy unboxing: Living in a (n unregulated) material world. *Media International Australia, 163*(1), 77–86.

Drenten, J., Gurrieri, L., & Tyler, M. (2020). Sexualized labour in digital culture: Instagram influencers, porn chic and the monetization of attention. *Gender, Work & Organization, 27*(1), 41–66.

Goanta, C., & Ranchordás, S. (Eds.). (2020). *The regulation of social media influencers* (pp. 1–22). Cheltenham, UK: Edward Elgar Publishing.

Gurkaynak, G., Kama, O., & Ergün, B. (2018). Navigating the uncharted risks of covert advertising in influencer marketing. *Business Law Review, 39*(1), 17–19.

Skiba, J., Petty, R. D., & Carlson, L. (2019). Beyond deception: Potential unfair consumer injury from various types of covert marketing. *Journal of Consumer Affairs, 53*(4), 1573–1601.

# 6
# BARRIERS AND CHALLENGES TO CONSIDER

How can a single tweet compromise online reputation? American skater Evan Lysacek was thought to nicely represent U.S. values.[1] That is until the figure skater decided to tweet disparagingly in reference to fellow skater Johnny Weir's gender identity. Following this post, his place as a role model and an influencer began unraveling. His sponsors at the time included Coca-Cola, AT&T, Ralph Lauren, Total Gym, Vera Wang, and Toyota.

Beyond the regulations surrounding influencers, there are other barriers and challenges to be considered. Paramount in this discussion is the role of authenticity. We look at the barriers and pressures that can make it harder for influencers and for brands to be effective. These include traditional endorser thinking and rules applied by third parties in the influencer context. We consider the risks and challenges for influencers, including both success stories (challenges overcome) and failures. Finally, we address ethical issues and dubious behaviors on the part of both influencers and brands that employ them.

The boundaries of and tensions within the influencer space are depicted in Figure 6.1. First, the tone and content of any communication are bounded by the macro context, which includes current events, prevailing trends, and relevant geopolitical and geosocial characteristics. Within the macro context, there may be industry, region, or personal specifics that set the stage for the sending and receiving of communications. Within these boundaries, there is a potential tension between the brand and the influencer, as well as influence on communications by third parties. Here, we are not examining governmental regulations but other sources of influence on the nature of communications. We look at each aspect of this model in turn.

DOI: 10.4324/9781003037767-6

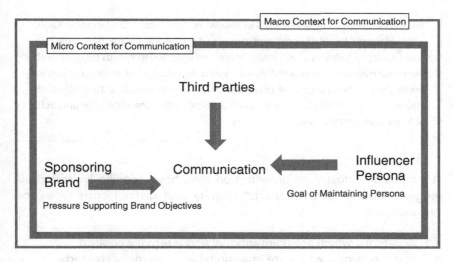

**FIGURE 6.1** Boundaries and Tensions Within the Influencer Space

## Macro and Micro Contextual Boundaries

Serious public events, such as the 2020 pandemic outbreak of the novel coronavirus, require communications that are sensitive to the context faced by many. Some brands cut budgets and canceled influencer campaigns, but those that continued could not be tone-deaf to suffering of their audience. Indeed, according to a 2020 study of those who follow influencers, reported by Global Web Index, people turned to influencers during the 2020 COVID-19 pandemic as a way to connect with someone at a time where they could not see friends and family in person. At the same time, consumers had greater expectations from brands to offer empathy, compassion, and authenticity, some or all of which influencers are known to provide.[2]

## SHIFTING GEARS IN A PANDEMIC

The global pandemic of 2020 saw marketing budgets by brands reduced; but, at the same time, spending by governments increased to support the response to COVID-19.[3] In the U.K., the same network that fought misinformation during the Ebola outbreak was employed to fight the misinformation regarding the Coronavirus. Social media influencers in this campaign included Bianca Gonzalez, a health expert and YouTube vlogger from the

Philippines with over seven million followers on Twitter; Dr. Jahangir Kabir, a Bangladeshi health expert and popular TV presenter with over one million Facebook followers; and @KlikDokter, an Indonesian health blogger with over four million Facebook followers.[4] Similarly, Finland has enlisted influencers in their efforts to control communication of the virus and to reach their citizens.[5] The central idea was to reach audiences disinterested in or unreachable by traditional channels.

A particular industry or organization may have specific limited challenges. Public relations experts[6] identify four distinct crisis types for organizations:

- Accidents, which are unintentional and internally created;
- Transgressions, which are intentional and internally created;
- Faux pas, which are unintentional and externally created;
- Terrorism, which is intentional and externally created.

Whether a macro or micro event, or a combination, marketers in fast-paced media are expected to provide fast-paced adaptation to circumstances. At the same time, bouncing marketing off a crisis faced by employees or attempting to profit from social unrest, such as that related to the "Black Lives Matter" movement, is typically met with repulsion. Moreover, the cataloguing of the "hellmouth of tone-deaf self-promotion" such as found at "influencersinthewild" is now commonplace within social media.[7]

## Authentic Communication

Influencer marketing has a natural tension between the brand sponsor and the influencer and their desire to maintain the persona (their public-facing characteristics) that made them attractive to the brand in the first place. This can arise from pressure applied by the sponsor to post brand-related communications, post frequently, or otherwise change the behavior that the influencer would have normally exhibited. Alternatively, tension may arise from the influencer's desire to monetize his or her potential while maintaining his or her persona and authenticity.

Straightforwardly, authenticity as a brand influencer is destroyed when statements, through commercial sponsorship, are no longer viewed as their own perspective but one warped by payment. Naturally, authenticity can be destroyed by behaviors aside from those linked to a brand. For example, Olivia Jade, daughter of designer Massimo Giannulli and actress Lori Loughlin, was reported to have lost followers in 2019, after documents identifying her college admissions fraud were disclosed.[8] Lori Loughlin and Massimo Giannulli subsequently pleaded guilty.[9] Following the scandal, Sephora Collection, a beauty brand, ended its partnership with Jade, as did several other companies.

One of the characteristics of influence is authenticity. But how is that authenticity developed, and then maintained or possibly destroyed? One reason brands partner with influencers is that they are "one of the few forms of real, authentic communication."[10] Actions that destroy influencer potential could be classified as intentional or unintentional and as originating with the brand or the influencer.

## Inauthentic Brands

In a case study set in Singapore,[11] several influencers hired by telecommunications provider SingTel and its agencies were disclosed for developing a campaign aimed to discredit competing brands (M1 and Starhub). In developing the campaign, Gushcloud, an influencer agency, engaged six influencers on behalf of SingTel to "badmouth rival telecom companies." Comments disparaging to rivals were posted until there was an anonymous leak of the campaign brief. As the writers noted, "This revelation was contentious because it was made public for the first time that even influencers' seemingly harmless and off-hand gripes against particular products and services could in fact be orchestrated advertorials."

The researchers report that influencers, attempting to recover credibility, took several paths. One influencer apologized and stated that the sponsorship by SingTel should have been noted in posts but also defended that the statements made regarding SingTel rivals were true. Another influencer noted that prior to joining the SingTel campaign, many posts against rival M1 had been made.

Without any intent to mislead, brands can push an influencer to the point of inauthenticity. Lifestyle blogger Chriselle Lim's post of her family posing with a Volvo appeared to be staged by the brand and was rejected as inauthentic by followers.[12]

## Inauthentic Influencers

One influencer couple, Marissa Fuchs and Gabriel Grossman, posted about a 3-day scavenger hunt that concluded with a marriage proposal. Followers turned on the couple when a marketing plan was discovered.[13] They were viewed as intending to dupe their followers.

In contrast, a well-known YouTube family, The Ingham Family, made a replica of their youngest child and sold the likeness of their child in collaboration with doll maker, Mary Shortle.[14] Some found the action fun, but others viewed it as overly commercial, even creepy. There was, however, no intentional deceit.

## Developing Authenticity

Authenticity in social media interactions has been found to support word-of-mouth recommendations and purchase likelihood.[15] Researchers[16] interested in the role of authenticity have developed four paths through which social media influencers manage authenticity. Through observations and interviews, they found three major signs of authenticity:

- creative content such as mini stories, often with pictures or videos;
- expressions of intrinsic satisfaction including emotions triggered by the product or service and the fit of the influencer with the product; and
- fact-based opinions.

---

**AUTHENTIC FROM THE ORIGIN**

Hydro Flask is best known for making insulated steel bottles that keep hot things hot and cold things cold. The company partnered with marketing agency, SocialWithin, to develop stories that featured their products and were true to their nature-loving, adventurous brand founded in Bend, Oregon. The goal of the campaign was to reach potential customers outside regions where they were already popular. Results over a 4-month period showed 12,000 purchases, an 80 percent increase in revenue, and a 16 times return on their advertising spending over the previous 4-month period.[17] Danny Veech, Account Manager with SocialWithin, stated: Ads in Instagram Stories has become one of our strongest-performing placements and has enabled Hydro Flask to reach significantly more of its ideal customers. We couldn't believe the results and have since changed our entire media buying and creative processes to optimize towards ads in Stories."[18]

---

The four pathways for authenticity management were argued to have varied levels of passion and transparency.

- *Fairytale authenticity* management is described as naive since it has a passion about products and services but lacks transparency about the commercial nature of posts. The thinking is that this unbridled enthusiasm may not ring true over time.

- *Disembodied authenticity* management discloses brand partnerships but lacks enthusiasm.
- *Fake authenticity* management posts without passion for the partnering brand, as if it were simply a job.
- *Absolute authenticity* management professionally combines passion for products and services of partner brands with transparency.

These researchers suggest that social media influencers must manage encroachment by brands to the content that makes them who they are. At the same time, it is in the brand's best interest that brand managers help influencers to preserve their authenticity. The tone should be one of coproduction that reduces creative constraints.

An emphasis on balance is reinforced by a study from the Netherlands.[19] In this work, 132 travel-oriented Instagram influencers were interviewed. The finding was that they needed to negotiate a tension: "they need to appear authentic, yet also approach their followers in a strategic way to remain appealing to advertisers."

Yet another study of travel influencers argues that there is an ethics of authenticity that people use when navigating difficult decisions regarding which brands to work with and what kind of content to produce for them.[20] These researchers found after interviewing 20 influencers that they have two concerns: being true to one's self and one's own brand, and being true to one's audience. One interviewee, in discussing the content he posts for his community, stated: "I cannot post something that doesn't fit in the community. Then I will be slaughtered in the comments." Another influencer experiencing conflict explains their tactic to cope: "You take the money because that's how you're making money now. As a traveler, I might not write about specific SIM cards for travelers in Malaysia, but they're offering me 300 USD so I write about it. But then maybe I post it and hide it, or I don't tweet it at times where I know the majority of my followers are going to see it." These researchers conclude that influencers, despite pressures, do engage in ethical decision-making in negotiating their content creation.

## Measuring Authenticity

Researchers[21] considering all kinds of horizontal partnerships, including sponsorship, influencer marketing, and brand placement, are interested in learning if the combination seems authentic.

Following the development of a brand authenticity scale,[22] a partner authenticity measure was developed on the basis of four characteristics:

- Continuity—the brand partnership is faithful to itself,
- Credibility—the brand partnership is true to its consumers,
- Integrity—the brand partnership is demonstrably motivated by care and responsibility, and
- Symbolism—the brand partnership supports consumers in being true to themselves.

A long, 16-item scale and a short, 4-item scale were developed and tested in sponsoring and in celebrity endorsement. As an example, these two scales work similarly in identifying how authentic the actress Jennifer Lawrence is as an endorser of the luxury brand Dior. With the long scale, a partner (influencer or brand) could check with its audience to see if the combination would be perceived as authentic before the relationship becomes a contract. In fact, a lack of one characteristic, such as integrity, might be identified and efforts put in place to demonstrate care and responsibility.

---

**AUTHENTIC GRANDPARENTS**

Worried about a dry cleaning business slowdown that was no fault of theirs, and with time on their hands, a sole proprietor couple in their eighties decided to follow their grandson's advice and post some photos on Instagram.[23] The couple from Taichung, Taiwan, have become an authentic social media hit around the world as they model clothes abandoned by clients. Ms. Hsu, aged 84 years, is noted as delivering a sort of haughty playfulness while Mr. Chang, aged 83 years, has a bit of swagger as they model fashion combinations that are eclectic by default. While they understand the Internet fame is fleeting, hope was there that someone would return for their clothes, and it did result in at least one person who had left garments over a year ago returning to collect them and pay his bill.[24]

---

## Third-Party Nongovernmental Barriers for Influencers

Influencers may be members of an organization, or may participate in an event, that limits their communication behavior. There is perhaps no better example here than the influence that the International Olympic Committee (IOC) holds over Olympic participants. IOC Rule 40 had in the past set forth a "blackout period" for participating athletes during the two weeks of the Olympics. The goal was to protect The Olympic Partner (TOP) sponsors, the dozen or so brands that held expensive contracts with the IOC, and make sure that their messages had no competition.

The harsh rule was amended by the IOC to read[25] "Competitors, team officials and other team personnel who participate in the Olympic Games may allow their person, name, picture, or sports performances to be used for advertising purposes during the Olympic Games in accordance with the principles determined by the IOC Executive Board." This ruling, which requires that athletes register their sponsor with their national Olympic committee, does permit athletes to communicate about a sponsor that has, for example, been supportive of them in the years leading up to their Olympic competition.

Another example of third-party barriers coming from sport was the U.S. prohibition of the National Collegiate Athletic Association (NCAA) for college athletes to earn money related in any way to their sport participation. Lawsuits over more than a decade have argued that athletes should have a right to their image and its uses; for example, when their likeness and style of play are featured in a video game.[26] Late in 2019, California became the first state to pass legislation allowing college athletes to be paid for endorsements and to hire their own sport agent representatives.

The NCAA responded to the California state bill, arguing that a change of this sort would destroy amateurism and wipe out the distinction between professional and college sports.[27] Nonetheless, other states followed suit, not wanting to be disadvantaged by states that did allow their athletes to be compensated for their name, likeness, and image.

The legal volleying continues, but the essence of changes to NCAA guidelines will not allow payment for sport participation; however, they will allow payments for social media promotions or product endorsements.[28] Athletes will be able to identify themselves as members of collegiate teams, but they will not be able to use intellectual property owned by the universities they represent. Many athletes already have substantial social media followings, so the changes will mean that they can now become paid influencers.

Third-party limitations on what can be communicated can also come from the social media platforms. For example, in enacting the FTC guidelines, YouTube requires influencers to put information about the relationship they have with a brand as an endorser in the actual video.[29] In sum, there are many ways in which what one might have said or done and posted might be influenced. These boundaries and tensions are part of the influencer world.

## Discussion Questions

1. Think of three influencers in terms of their authenticity. How authentic do you find them to be, and how does that impact your reaction to the brands they promote?
2. Have you encountered influencers who seem highly inauthentic to you? What made you feel that way? Did you do any further research to try to confirm the authenticity of their posts?
3. Look at the content posted by two influencers you are not already following. Consider the three major signs of authenticity (creative content, fit with product, and fact-based opinions), and determine how well these influencers display these signals.
4. Do you think college athletes should be allowed to serve as influencers for brands (currently under discussion by NCAA)? Why or why not?

## Notes

1. Colapinto, C., & Benecchi, E. (2014). The presentation of celebrity personas in everyday twittering: Managing online reputations throughout a communication crisis. *Media, Culture & Society, 36*(2), 219–233.
2. Global Web Index, The Age of Influence, 2020.
3. www.prnewsonline.com/PSA-government-influencers-coronavirus
4. www.socialmediatoday.com/news/the-uk-government-is-partnering-with-social-media-influencers-to-combat-cov/574129/
5. www.theguardian.com/world/2020/apr/01/finland-enlists-social-influencers-in-fight-against-covid-19
6. Coombs, W. T., & Holladay, S. J. (1996). Communication and attributions in a crisis: An experimental study in crisis communication. *Journal of Public Relations Research, 8*(4), 279–295.
7. https://www.vanityfair.com/style/2020/06/behold-the-influencers-using-blacklivesmatter-to-enhance-their-personal-brands
8. https://wwd.com/fashion-news/fashion-scoops/lori-loughlin-mossimo-giannulli-college-fraud-scandal-olivia-jade-influencer-1203083757/
9. https://www.washingtonpost.com/
10. Scott, D. M. (2015). *The new rules of marketing and P.R.: How to use social media, online video, mobile applications, blogs, news releases, and viral marketing to reach buyers directly* (p. 295). Hoboken, NJ: John Wiley & Sons.
11. Abidin, C., & Ots, M. (2016). Influencers tell all. *Blurring the Lines*, 153.
12. https://izea.com/2019/03/04/influencer-marketing-gone-wrong/
13. www.insider.com/instagram-stars-insist-sponsored-wedding-proposal-was-surprise-to-bride-2019-6
14. www.insider.com/youtuber-family-selling-life-like-replica-dolls-of-newborn-baby-2019-7
15. Kowalczyk, C. M., & Pounders, K. R. (2016). Transforming celebrities through social media: The role of authenticity and emotional attachment. *Journal of Product & Brand Management, 25*(4), 345–356.

16. Audrezet, A., De Kerviler, G., & Moulard, J. G. (2020). Authenticity under threat: When social media influencers need to go beyond self-presentation. *Journal of Business Research, 117*, 557–569.
17. https://business.instagram.com/success/hydro-flask
18. Ibid.
19. van Driel, L., & Dumitrica, D. (2020). Selling brands while staying "Authentic": The professionalization of Instagram influencers. *Convergence*, 1354856520902136.
20. Wellman, M. L., Stoldt, R., Tully, M., & Ekdale, B. (2020). Ethics of authenticity: Social media influencers and the production of sponsored content. *Journal of Media Ethics, 35*(2), 68–82.
21. Charlton, A. B., & Cornwell, T. B. (2019). Authenticity in horizontal marketing partnerships: A better measure of brand compatibility. *Journal of Business Research, 100*, 279–298.
22. Morhart, F., Malär, L., Guèvremont, A., Girardin, F., & Grohmann, B. (2015). Brand authenticity: An integrative framework and measurement scale. *Journal of Consumer Psychology, 25*(2), 200–218.
23. www.nytimes.com/2020/07/24/world/asia/taiwan-octogenarian-couple-instagram-laundry.html?referringSource=articleShare
24. Ibid.
25. www.olympic.org/news/commercial-opportunities-for-participants-during-the-olympic-games-tokyo-2020-presented
26. Holthaus, W. D., Jr. (2010). Ed O'Bannon v. NCAA: Do former NCAA athletes have a case against the NCAA for its use of their likenesses. *Louis ULJ, 55*, 369.
27. www.ncaa.org/about/resources/media-center/news/ncaa-responds-california-senate-bill-206
28. www.insidehighered.com/news/2020/04/30/ncaa-board-governors-approves-name-image-likeness-guidelines
29. https://adespresso.com/blog/influencer-marketing-guidelines/

## Further Reading

Abidin, C. (2016). "Aren't these just young, rich women doing vain things online?": Influencer selfies as subversive frivolity. *Social Media + Society, 2*(2), 1–17.

Arriagada, A., & Concha, P. (2019). Cultural intermediaries in the making of branded music events: Digital cultural capital in tension. *Journal of Cultural Economy*, 1–12.

Cornwell, T. B. (2019). Less "sponsorship as advertising" and more sponsorship-linked marketing as authentic engagement. *Journal of Advertising, 48*(1), 49–60.

Jin, S. V., Muqaddam, A., & Ryu, E. (2019). Instafamous and social media influencer marketing. *Marketing Intelligence & Planning, 37*(5), 567–579.

Lou, C., & Yuan, S. (2019). Influencer marketing: How message value and credibility affect consumer trust of branded content on social media. *Journal of Interactive Advertising, 19*(1), 58–73.

Nistor, C., Yalcin, T., & Pehlivan, E. (2018). Duplicity in alternative marketing communications. *Markets, Globalization & Development Review, 3*(2), Article 4.

# 7

# HOW INFLUENCE IS MEASURED AND EVALUATED

The old adage about a tree falling in the forest and nobody hearing it applies to the world of influencer marketing. If personas are selected or developed to promote a brand but nobody measures the outcome properly, there may have been influence but the marketer will not learn of it and this may dictate their future decisions regarding the approach. Influencer marketing, when done well, fits inside a much larger advertising, media, and marketing ecosystem. That means that, just as brands need to evaluate their creative messages or the impact of their TV dollars or their sports sponsorships, so do they need to measure and appraise how well their influencer marketing strategies work. A company or brand that does not put a comprehensive measurement plan in place for this element of its marketing budget will likely struggle to achieve success. Or, if they are lucky enough to succeed one time, it will be challenging to replicate because they will not know why it worked.

This chapter considers current measurement approaches, including the relatively few syndicated offerings, some alternatives to the mainstream, and what the future of measurement could look like. It concludes with thoughts on measurement management.

The first challenge for marketers in terms of measuring influencers happens at the beginning—that is, finding the right influencer for a given brand. Initiating an influencer contract starts with key brand marketing objectives, not simply trying to get the highest numbers (reach) of a specific target group or a general population. Marketers need to ensure that the influencer's style is aligned with the brand so that the message does not sound forced.[1]

DOI: 10.4324/9781003037767-7

## FINDING THE RIGHT INFLUENCER VIA SOCIAL LISTENING

Social listening uses online technology to identify keywords of interest on the Internet generally but in particular on social media. There are many free sources on platforms and paid services that may be general or platform specific. A plethora of social listening tools are available such as Netbase and Brandwatch (general listening tools), BuzzSumo and Followerwonk (for Twitter), and Traackr (focuses on influencers in their database but names can be added). Social listening can help in identifying organic influencers, individuals already talking about or using a brand. It can also identify influencers already working with competitor brands and monitor ongoing conversations that may include brands, keywords, and hashtags of interest.

## Followers and Friends

As is often the case when a new promotional opportunity is created, marketers may choose to assess effects by using existing tools and approaches. Such is the case with influencer marketing. Since it originated as an extension of (and hybrid between) word of mouth and social media, the easiest way to gauge it has been to look at the number of followers or friends that an individual influencer generates. Indeed, the foundational definition of whether an influencer is classified as "macro" or "micro" is based on these numbers. The macro influencer is someone who has 10,000 or more followers, whereas the micro influencer has fewer than that minimum.

Beauty influencer Huda Kattan (#hudabeauty), for example, has more than 42 million followers. The Brothers Buoy (#thebrothersbuoy) post about the best places to eat in Brooklyn, New York, to their more than 11,000 followers. On Facebook, 6.7 million people have liked (friended) Huda Beauty, and 280 have liked The Brothers Buoy. But what do all those numbers really mean? Would the Buoy Brothers' promotion of Diplomatic Rum be ineffective because their numbers are much lower than Huda's? If someone follows an influencer or friends them on Facebook, what does that mean in terms of brand impact? One can argue that those actions, in and of themselves, indicate an interest in what those influencers are talking about, and a willingness to be associated with them. But for most brands, this sheer "count" merely provides a way to classify and categorize the influencers as macro or micro.

One of the more recent challenges with relying on counts of followers to estimate the value of an influencer is that of online fraud. As noted in Chapter 5, fraud occurs when robots (bots) are counted as "followers" even though they are not actual people. This leads to a concern in the industry that the influencer investment is hollow. Fraud can take the form of fake followers, fake likes, or fake influence that is suggested when influencers do not properly disclose their connection to a brand. All of these threaten to damage the authenticity between influencers and those who follow them, which goes against the key value that influencers bring to brands.

The 2019 decision by Instagram to remove the number of likes on posts will likely result in influencers being assessed more by performance metrics than the vanity measure of how many people like their content.[2] The removal of this metric, it is hoped, will reduce the kind of influencer fraud as noted earlier.

## Engagement and Tracking

For marketers, the connection between an influencer and his or her audience needs to be stronger than the simple count of followers or friends. One way to measure the importance of an influencer is by how many of his or her followers have taken an additional action and engaged in some way with the content posted by the influencer. Marketers typically have brand-specific funnels, or progression in engagement, that they believe individuals follow, such as exposure, awareness, knowledge, preference, and purchase, even repeat purchase or loyalty.

The first measures marketers look at here are retweets and shares. Combined, they represent an amplification of the influencer's voice, extending it to additional people. According to Shareablee, one of the companies that continuously measure social media impact, the total volume of consumer actions on social media hit 74 billion in 2019, a 4 percent increase over the prior year. Influencers accounted for 33 percent of the content posted on social media and fully 74 percent of the actions.[3] There is an interesting distinction in consumer engagement with an influencer's post about a brand and the brand's own posts. For example, JetBlue Airways found it had an average of 2,363 engagements on the posts it released, compared to the average 241,226 engagements with its influencers' posts.[4]

Beyond counts of engagement, marketers can have influencers include a tracking pixel (a small piece of software code) in their posts which, when clicked by the viewer or follower, go to a separate landing page for the brand that can then be tracked specifically. While regular Instagram posts do not allow this since everything on a post must be self-contained within Instagram, the same is not true of Instagram Stories, which are able to include links. If marketers place a pixel in the link then they can measure how many unique users go on to their website from the Instagram Story. In this way, linking through Stories helps drive a brand's lower-funnel results, such as site visits, product purchase, or coupon delivery and redemption. This is in contrast to how most marketers use influencers, to drive the upper funnel measures such as brand awareness and preference. Now, engagement can be measured not only in and of itself, but also more tangibly in how it drives quantifiable brand results.

Another important way to measure engagement with brands as a result of influencer activity is through consumer surveys. This was the approach taken by Kraft Heinz for an influencer campaign called #Love-ForKraft. Kraft used macro and micro influencers for an Instagram campaign that drove brand awareness, favorability, and intent. They wanted to measure the impact of the #LoveforKraft campaign on perceptions of the Kraft brand. Kraft's influencers were all parents who had responded to earlier campaigns. The company invited the top performers to be part of the #LoveforKraft program. They were told to buy their favorite Kraft products and feature them in their Instagram posts at least two times per month, for which they each received a $75 Visa gift card. Research was conducted to compare people who had been exposed to the #LoveforKraft campaign on Instagram with a control, unexposed group. Those who were exposed had to have some knowledge of the influencers. That group had 173 people, compared to the 200 in the control group. The research found that those exposed to the campaign were more favorable to Kraft, had higher awareness (both unaided and top of mind), and higher ratings of brand attributes among those who did not have children or were not regular Kraft buyers. Unaided awareness was 77 percent for those exposed to the campaign as compared to 61 percent for those not exposed. Brand favorability was 66 percent for those exposed compared to 51 percent among the control.[5]

More broadly, consumers self-report that they are influenced to take actions following influencer posts. In a survey conducted in 2019 with 2,767 people in the U.S. and 3,568 in the U.K., nearly one in five (17 percent) of Internet users in the U.S. and the U.K. said they were inspired to buy something after seeing an influencer or celebrity post on social media. For those in Gen Z, the proportion was higher, at 22 percent.[6]

## Social Measurement Tools

Not surprisingly, the growth and development of social media has been followed by companies offering measurement services. Some are offered by the influencer platforms themselves, such as Google and

Facebook. Both Google and Facebook provide extensive analytics within their respective platforms (including YouTube and Instagram, respectively). The Facebook Brand Collabs Manager is a tool within its site that helps brands find influencers. Facebook has added Instagram to this tool.[7]

Others come from third-party companies that have seized on the opportunity to fill the gap. These include Kred, InfluencerDB, PeerIndex (owned by Brandwatch), and Netbase. These tools can help marketers understand not only the number of followers, but also the number of engagements. A potential influencer's metrics should be compared to those of the competitors. Social sentiment is important too, to ensure that consumers have not gone from highly positive engagement with the brand or influencer, to the opposite.[8]

One social measurement company, Netbase, which is a global analytics platform that helps marketers understand consumer conversations online, differentiates influencers from brand ambassadors. The former are those who have an expertise in a particular field (fitness, beauty, sports, etc.) and talk about specific brands that they like, while the latter are those whom brands sometimes pay to talk about them specifically. Mercedez-Benz employs brand influencers on Instagram to help drive awareness of its brand. They have done so, in part, through the hashtag #MBFanPhoto, which solicits people to share pictures of their cars. Many brands combine their brand ambassador program, which relies on (unpaid) employees and customers, with paid influencers. Lululemon, for example, encourages people who like the brand to post on social media, in addition to fitness influencers such as professional surfer Malia Manuel or NFL player Nick Foles.

Most social media monitoring tools have basic counts of key indicators, but several focus on the delivery of a particular insight. Examples include Hootsuite, a flexible and free software platform that can help to schedule posts across platforms; Keyhole, a program that allows real-time understanding of hashtags, key words and name use; and Digimind, a social media listening platform that emphasizes sentiment and insights monitoring. The list goes on and on: Brandwatch, Talkwalker, Reputology, Synthesio, Mentionlytics, Nuzzel, Crowd Analyzer, Nexology, and Tweepsmap.[9] The point is that if there is a measurement need, there is likely a program tailored for it, with more cropping up all the time.

When we talk about measurement, we have to consider its value and importance from two distinct but interrelated perspectives. The influencers are eager to track how well they are doing, both individually and compared to others in the same category. Ingrid Nilsen, a beauty influencer with her own YouTube channel (Missglamorazzi), monitors how many Instagram followers and YouTube subscribers she has relative to others in the beauty arena. Are her 1.3 million Instagram followers and 3.8 million subscribers larger than those of other beauty influencers? And are her numbers trending up or down?

## Measurement From the Influencer Perspective

Most everyday influencers are tracking their counts of followers or likes. They want to manage their content so that it draws in more people, which in turn could encourage advertisers to pay them (or pay them more) to promote particular brands. By closely monitoring their posts, they can learn which ones are more or less appealing and engaging. Does Kayla Itsines's post on a new exercise lead to more Instagram shares or YouTube likes than a post about fitness clothing? Are the followers of travel influencer Jack Morris more engaged with his posts about Cambodia than Paris? Is there a time sensitivity to the posts? That is, does content posted on weekdays perform better than that on weekends (or vice versa)? Or is the time of day important in terms of generating attention and action among followers? As influencer marketing occurs in digital channels, every response can be tracked. Further, since people have to register to use these platforms, the influencers can know not only how many followers they have but also some basic (aggregated) information about them, such as age or gender. James Charles, for example, the first male spokesmodel for Cover Girl cosmetics, might be interested to learn what percentage of his Instagram followers are male.

Influencers do have their own preferences on the kinds of measurement they would like from brands they work with. While brands are most likely to want to measure engagement and/or reach, the influencers want to start with clearly laid-out goals of what the brand is expecting from them so that the measurement can be put against the stated goal. They are also interested in creating longer-term deals in order to develop a proper partnership with the brand, and play more of an advocacy and education role with their audiences, rather than just trying to sell a "widget."[10]

## Measurement From the Brand Perspective

While the fact that all that the influencer is interested in measuring is also of value to brands, the crux of an advertiser's interest in measuring influencer marketing is in understanding the Return on Investment (ROI) of the dollars that they are spending in this way. That is, what marketers want to know is, for every dollar that they invest in influencer marketing (i.e., paying to an influencer to promote their specific brand), how much do they get in return? If it is less than the dollar invested, the marketer may want to reassess the value, but if it is significantly more than that dollar, then maybe more should be invested in this way. That sounds very practical. The challenge, however, is determining the return generated specifically by this investment. This is the case not just for influencer marketing; it is actually quite difficult for marketers to measure ROI for all of the channels that they use.

ROI is calculated using sophisticated statistical marketing mix models. They are typically based on some form of regression, using historical data to predict what will happen in the future. Traditionally, data that is included captures some kind of audience metric, such as a TV rating or a radio rating. Where ratings have not been available, traffic counts have been incorporated. In addition to an advertiser's own marketing and media spend, these models usually include what has been done by the competitive brands, as well as broader data that could impact the response, such as weather patterns, economic indicators, or consumer confidence. The challenge these models have had is twofold. First, they rely on historical data, which makes it hard to account for ongoing changes in the environment that could alter how consumers might react to the marketing mix in the future. Second, they have looked at the holistic impact of a particular mix of media (and channels), rather than being able to break down the underlying elements to show how they have worked together to deliver ROI.

As a result, marketers moved some of their attention in measurement to more granular Multi-Touch Attribution Models (MTA) that not only make forecasts but also show the interrelationships of the parts, helping marketers to understand whether, for example, it was the TV ad that drove search, or a digital ad, and how all of that led to a store visit and then a sale.

It is not common, but sometimes a brand with little other concurrent advertising can use their influencer campaign to gain meaningful measurement of impact. In 2018, Liquid Plumr, a brand of drain cleaner, engaged YouTube creators Vat19 to use the "Will it Clog?" format to test the product in action.[11] The product was used to unplug weird clogs from chocolates to bacon grease, generating three million organic views in the first weekend and immediate sales growth from September 2018 to well into 2019.[12]

In influencer marketing, these models have generally not yet been developed sufficiently to provide an insight on which elements of the practice are driving a sale of the promoted brand. Since the audience data that is measured for influencer marketing has primarily been combined with all other digital audience measures (clicks, views, completion rates), we do not yet fully understand the specific relationship between influencers' followers or shares or retweets and consumer response to the brand message. This is an area ripe for further exploration. While measurement is happening on a case-by-case or campaign-by-campaign basis, it has not yet been examined more broadly.

There is another measurement consideration for brands as far as influencer marketing is concerned, and that is the potential impact on the overall business. That is, while marketers are still trying to determine the tangible ROI of influencers, they must also consider the negative potential of the practice. Casper Sleep, a mattress company that sells directly to consumers, noted in its filing for an initial public offering that influencers could in fact be a business liability, stating "if we were held responsible for the content of their posts, we could be forced to alter our practices."[13]

While most measurement that brands need relates to the outcome and impact of influencer activity, there is an increasing number of software platforms being developed to help brands find the right influencers. The software can look at potential influencers in terms of their reach and engagement levels. Stargazer is one such example, working with several million influencers that companies can filter to find the best one for their needs. Brandwatch is another company that offers different tools to help marketers find influencers. All the people it has compiled into its influencer database of 450,000 people have been given an Influence Score, based on the levels of engagement with them. Its BuzzSumo service allows users to search for content shared on a topic to see who shared it, or simply find an influencer by looking at keywords and hashtags.[14]

How marketers measure the success of their influencer campaigns remains a challenge, according to a survey by Linqia, with seven in ten (71 percent) of responding companies saying that engagement was the key. Other highly valued measures used included upper-funnel metrics such as brand awareness or sentiment and lower-funnel measures like conversions, clicks, and sales. At the same time, when asked about the key concerns about their influencer programs, the most frequently mentioned one was the ability to measure the ROI of such programs.[15] Similar responses were seen in a 2019 survey of marketers conducted by Inmar. Here, 85 percent of marketers agreed that they used engagement data as the main measure of success for influencer marketing, while nearly two-thirds (59 percent) reported they used social traffic (visits to social media apps) for measurement. Four in ten (40 percent) relied on follower counts to determine success. Tracking effectively was listed as the key to measuring influencer marketing by the Forbes Agency Council, which noted that putting a good tracking mechanism in place was the first thing that a marketer should do when hiring an influencer for its brand.[16]

---

**EXPERTS SHARE EXPERTISE**

Eleven members of the Forbes Agency Council were asked for their view on how to measure influencer ROI.[17] Following is a summary of their thoughts.

1. Measure channel performance by attributing a sale back to the influencer—for example, through the use of a promotional code.
2. Read direct comments from consumers in an influencer's posts to see if there is any interest in the product.
3. Track everything that contributes to a sale such as shares, likes, and comments.
4. Look beyond vanity metrics such as impressions and consider brand lift in awareness and perceptions.
5. Determine your desired outcome and, before engaging with an influencer, go after those with proven outcomes similar to the ones you seek.
6. Request regular reports that give a qualitative feeling of how things are going for the brand.
7. Create custom tracking for each influencer with whom you work so that their cost-per-click, cost-per-action, or cost-per-install (such as in a game download) can be evaluated.
8. Utilize influencer analytics platforms and set up your key performance indicators so that they are easily translatable into your ROI.
9. Implement measurable trigger points like unique landing pages to learn about influencer performance.
10. Utilize unique codes or even a special product that is only available to followers or subscribers of your influencer.
11. Create separate affiliate links for an influencer that will not only track things like clicks but also abandon carts, email captures, or sales.

---

## Academic Measurement

Planning models that optimize influencer communications are being developed to solve selection and scheduling challenges. For example, a model for a short-horizon campaign has been put forward that considers each of the following:

- An influencer's network size and the strength of influence,
- Any network overlap between multiple influencers, and
- Multiple exposure effects that might arise from peer-to-peer sharing.[18]

The goal of these optimizing models is to make the most of a constrained budget.

A very different approach was taken in understanding the factors that impact YouTube influencer credibility. Researchers asked 497 YouTube viewers a slate of questions about influencer expertise, trustworthiness, likability, homophily (how similar the influencer is to the viewer), social advocacy, interactivity, argument quality, involvement, knowledge, and attitude toward the video and brand.[19] They found that trustworthiness, social influence, argument quality, and information involvement were important if the YouTube influencer is to be perceived as credible and the video likable.[20]

Measurement of influencer marketing presents challenges in the melding of quantitative big data and qualitative understanding. Quantitative measures are abundant to the point of being overwhelming, but often not informative in the way managers would like. The main question is typically how to capture the conversion from a like or share to the decision to buy a brand. The beauty of influencer marketing—a single, informed voice telling the brand story—is also its largest challenge in measurement. Currently, there is no one-size-fits-all measure. Likewise, ROI calculations require connectivity between influencer actions and audience-brand behaviors. Here lies the paradox of influencer marketing. People share and reshare interesting posts, sometimes adding up to millions of data points. Yet, we are still working to understand how to properly connect an ultimate purchase decision with the originating influence.

## Managers and Measurement

Influencers and their supporting teams may also be hired as social media managers in terms of developing strategy and content and managing interactions with their followers.[21] This role suggests that they may be able to measure, report, and interpret important outcomes of a campaign to the brand manager. Comparing the extent to which this self-study by an influencer aligns with commercially supplied data is one approach to insight and confirmation.

It is also important to understand what measures managers use and how they use them. In a study conducted in Germany, social media managers were asked to evaluate quantitative and qualitative key performance indicators.[22] Managers were initially drawn to quantitative measures such as the number of post interactions, firm performance (e.g., sales), and influencer followers. However, when pressed to make trade-offs among metrics, they turned to the net sentiment of user comments (the number of positive comments minus the number of negative comments). The findings suggest that managers use readily available count metrics, but, when the more nuanced sentiment metrics are available, those receive greater attention and interest.

Clearly, the measurement for influencer marketing is a work in progress. Marketers will continue to look for ways to evaluate the potential of each influencer they consider or use, as well as try to assess the impact of that influencer on brand success, while the influencers themselves will search for the best metrics to demonstrate their impact on the brand. It is a never-ending dance that will evolve as influencer marketing itself continues to develop.

## Discussion Questions

1. How important is it to consumers to know the number of followers an influencer has? Does Instagram's removal of the number of likes to an influencer's post make a difference to how you perceive the influencer?
2. Why do you think influencers' posts about a brand typically generate far more engagement than the brand's own posts?
3. What measures should an influencer care most about? Which ones are of less importance?
4. If you were asked to advise a brand on influencer measurement, what would you recommend?
5. Should influencers be used more to drive brand awareness and consideration (so-called "upper-funnel" measures) than to drive brand sales ("lower-funnel" measures)? Why or why not?
6. How much should marketers rely on software platforms to help them select the right influencer to work with?
7. Is there any downside to influencer marketing measurement relying primarily on data analysis of social media activity (posts, likes, shares, etc.)?

## Notes

1. Williamson, D. A. (2017, January). Measuring influencer marketing: A guide for marketers. *eMarketer*.
2. Influencer Marketing. (2019). *Global web index trend report*. Retrieved from www.globalwebindex.com
3. Shareablee, Year in Review, 2019.
4. Influencer Marketing Roundup. *eMarketer*, March 2018.
5. "#LoveForKraft Influencer Marketing Campaign," Case Study.
6. "Influencer Marketing," Global Web Index Trend Report 2019.
7. Hutchinson, A. (2019, December 18). Facebook expands brand collabs manager to include Instagram creators. *Social Media Today*.

8. *Netbase: The 2019 complete guide to influencer marketing.* Retrieved from www.netbase.com
9. https://blog.hootsuite.com/social-media-monitoring-tools/
10. Williamson, D. A. (2020, March). Influencer marketing and the path to purchase. *eMarketer.*
11. Neff, J. (2020). Unclogging liquid plumr sales. *Advertising Age, 91*(5), 24.
12. Ibid.
13. Williamson, D. A. (2020, March). Influencer marketing and the path to purchase. *eMarketer.*
14. You're measuring influencer marketing wrong. *Collective Bias.* Retrieved from www.collectivebias.com
15. Linquia: The State of Influencer Marketing 2020.
16. Seven ways to track ROI for influencer marketing. *Forbes Agency Council*, March 17, 2019, 1–4. Retrieved from www.forbes.com/sites/forbesagencycouncil/2018
17. www.forbes.com/sites/forbesagencycouncil/2020/06/04/11-ways-to-measure-influencer-marketing-roi/#7b8afb2c2c75
18. Mallipeddi, R., Kumar, S., Sriskandarajah, C., & Zhu, Y. (2018). A framework for analyzing influencer marketing in social networks: Selection and scheduling of influencers. *Fox School of Business Research Paper*, 18–42.
19. Xiao, M., Wang, R., & Chan-Olmsted, S. (2018). Factors affecting YouTube influencer marketing credibility: A heuristic-systematic model. *Journal of Media Business Studies, 15*(3), 188–213.
20. Ibid.
21. Campbell, C., & Farrell, J. R. (2020). More than meets the eye: The functional components underlying influencer marketing. *Business Horizons*, forthcoming.
22. Gräve, J. F., & Greff, A. (2018, July). Good KPI, good influencer? Evaluating success metrics for social media influencers. In *Proceedings of the 9th international conference on social media and society* (pp. 291–295).

## Further Reading

Arora, A., Bansal, S., Kandpal, C., Aswani, R., & Dwivedi, Y. (2019). Measuring social media influencer index-insights from Facebook, Twitter and Instagram. *Journal of Retailing and Consumer Services, 49*, 86–101.
Barhorst, J. B., Wilson, A., & Brooks, J. (2020). Negative Tweets and their impact on likelihood to recommend. *Journal of Business Research, 117*, 727–739.
Martínez-López, F. J., Anaya-Sánchez, R., Fernández Giordano, M., & Lopez-Lopez, D. (2020). Behind influencer marketing: Key marketing decisions and their effects on followers' responses. *Journal of Marketing Management, 36*(7–8), 579–607.
Sciarrino, J., Wilcox, G. B., & Chung, A. (2020). Measuring the effectiveness of peer-to-peer influencer marketing in an integrated brand campaign. *Journal of Digital & Social Media Marketing, 8*(1), 85–95.

# 8

# THE FUTURE FOR INFLUENCERS

When data was first published on how much influencers were being paid, with celebrities such as Kylie Jenner earning more than $1 million per post, many believed that the future for influencer marketing pointed in just one direction—up. Business Insider's *Influencer Marketing* report predicted the influencer marketing industry would be worth more than $15 billion in 2022 as compared to $8 billion in 2019.[1] But other voices started to question the solidity of the future of influencer marketing, wondering whether intermittent scandals, from the implosion of the Fyre Festival to the fabrication of cancer by Belle Gibson to the deception of race by Emma Hallberg[2] have eroded consumers' trust, and without trust there is little in the way of influence. Casey Ferrell, Vice President and Head of research firm U.S. Monitor, has said "We are at peak influencer, and it's beginning to run its course."[3] Whether that downward trajectory is only with celebrity influencers, rather than peer or micro influencers, remains to be seen.

The two views, one of decline and one of growth, may in fact be reconcilable. This chapter looks at trends that shape influencer marketing, current areas of concern, and areas of future research.

## Digital Media and the Influencer

The prediction for an expanding role for influencers can be made in part on expansion of their natural habitat, namely streaming online. Television viewing has experienced a steady decline, even if more slowly than some predicted. In the U.S., average ratings for popular primetime broadcast programs that used to be in the high double digits are now

DOI: 10.4324/9781003037767-8

routinely under 5 percent. The way that U.S. viewers receive and watch videos has been changing rapidly. Between 2014 and 2018, the percentage of U.S. households having cable, satellite, or Telco services fell from 84 to 74 percent. At the same time, penetration of streaming services went from 50 percent to 75 percent of households.[4]

In the U.S., the most popular streaming service is YouTube, with 164 million monthly active users toward the end of 2019.[5] Twitch streaming estimated their 2019 users to be 37.5 million but to grow to 47 million by 2023.[6] Perhaps as importantly, Twitch reports having 3 million active monthly content creators and 15 million daily streamers.[7] By the end of March 2020, Nielsen reported a more than doubling in the weekly total minutes of streaming content viewed, as well as an increase in the share of total viewing attributed to streamed content versus traditional broadcast or cable services.[8]

One can also see from the recent advance of TikTok that there may be more mobile streamed services on the horizon. TikTok was introduced in 2016 and in the U.S. in 2017 and has gained 14.3 million users.[9] Quibi, introduced in 2020, gained nearly half a million subscribers in its first week. Additionally, new streaming TV offerings from Walt Disney (Disney+), Apple (Apple TV+), WarnerMedia (HBO Max), and NBC Universal (Peacock) are not only focused on TV-like broadcasting but also recognize the potential for greater future interactivity than traditional, one-way broadcasting.[10]

## AI INFLUENCERS

Miquela Sousa is 100 percent computer generated and discussed as one of the most financially successful AI influencers in terms of brand relationships.[11] "Lil Miquela" not only represents brands like Prada and UGGs on Instagram but is seen on billboards from England to Japan.[12] Her persona is carefully crafted with passages such as this: "I really played myself this time. One of angel boi's friends told him who I was and he saw everything I've been posting about him. He blew up at me over lunch and stormed out as I ugly cried in front of about 50 strangers . . . and now he won't respond to any of texts or pick up his phone. Y'all were right ~ I should have just told him the truth. It just felt so good to have someone like me for me . . . but I guess that wasn't even true, because who I am on here IS me. My heart feels like it's short-circuiting and on 1% battery all at once. Brb crying to Lana for the next 19 years" posted to Instagram.[13] Buying into the narrative also comes with a picture of Miquela's face streaked with eye make-up from her tears. Many will argue that she is the future of influencer marketing and that brands will create their own avatars.

## The Integration of Influence and Content Production

As the Internet expanded, it opened up the opportunity for individuals, brands, and organizations of all kinds to develop a presence or even a channel. Pretty soon, the phrase "content is king" became popular, in recognition of the fact that with so many more outlets available, the key to attracting and retaining viewers or followers lies in creating excellent content. What quickly followed was the realization that it was challenging to continue feeding the "content monster." Posting a blog was easy, setting up a YouTube channel was simple, and garnering initial interest was possible, but maintaining all of that was an entirely different thing. Brands and media companies seeking to target their communications effectively in digital media understood the value in creating lifestyle or geographically focused channels, but their ability to fill these channels with up-to-date and relevant content was time-consuming and expensive. Increasingly, that content has been supplied by influencers.

One way in which the content void is filled is by prosumers (people who are a producer and a consumer at the same time).[14] User-generated content is when consumers interact with the product or service and create content in this process. Nowhere is this more evident than in sport. Take the example of the "RallytheWorld" campaign utilized by Volkswagen Motorsport at the FIA World Rally Championship. This social media campaign utilized transmedia storytelling that built relationships with fans and between fans.[15] A digital hub supported transmedia storytelling for the fan community. The Volkswagen social media campaigner explains that the hub

> provides the global fan base with access to the circuits, challenges, and team pilots. A social media buzz, mobile gaming, live events and competitions ensure the fans get a piece of the action—and keep coming back for more for over twelve months. These fan events are equally spectacular as the championship itself: whether the search for a helmet holder, voting for the perfect fan food, or being one of the 4,000 faces on the Fan Car as a photo stuck to the Polo R WRC [World Rally Championship car build by Volkswagen].[16]

A study published by Obviously, an influencer marketing agency, finds influencers have become pseudo-production agencies.[17] Highlights from their study of their influencers found that:

- Brands hire influencers to create their photo and video assets,
- Influencers are more cost-effective than hiring a creative agency to do the work, and
- Influencer-created content is more successful on social media.

Even for some not intending to be influencers, social media content production has become essential to career development. For example, professional rock climbers feel the production and distribution of new media content is imperative to their climbing careers.[18] In effect, in order to have a successful career, they must become brand ambassadors.[19]

We can see the importance of content and the management of personal image in rule changes made by the National Collegiate Athletic Association (NCAA) regarding the rights of athletes. As noted in Chapter 6, the NCAA rule change allows college athletes to earn money from endorsements and sponsorship deals, likely in 2021, that had been prohibited for students.[20] Some of the discussion focuses on players having the right to earn money from their names, images, and likenesses, but, importantly, the rule change will also give college athletes the right to develop influencer personas. In fact, the acronym "NILI" is becoming commonplace to refer to Name, Image, Likeness, and Influence.[21] If athletes start to develop a following and gain experience managing their self-presentation early, before their professional sports career begins, then their long-term value may be greater.

In sum, the expansion of streaming, the demand for content, and the changing character of self-presentation suggest that influencer marketing may well expand. There are, however, countervailing forces that may lead it to develop differently over time.

## What Remains in Flux

### Children and Influence

There continues to be significant social unease about children as targets of influence, and as influencers themselves. For example, the ability of vloggers (video bloggers) to reach children with their interactive games, toy unboxing videos, product reviews, and to influence their brand preferences is of increasing concern.[22] Another area to monitor is in the targeting of adolescents with unhealthy foods. In a Flemish study of 21 adolescents aged 12–18 years, researchers found that their social media was filled with food messages put forward by peer influencers.[23]

Children who post on social media regarding products and services are now being referred to as "kidfluencers." BrandTrends explains that large companies like Walmart are utilizing child vloggers to reach targets and boost their social media impact. BrandTrends mentions Evan-Tube as an example, a child having a combined YouTube, Facebook, Twitter, and Instagram following of over 10 million. This leads to questions of whether children as young as 4 or 5 years should be spending significant time marketing products and services.

## Social Good and Well-Being

It was once thought that meaningful social interactions, for example with family members, were replaced by social technology leading to reduced psychological well-being.[24] Subsequently, research on the outcomes of Internet communications suggested that the "rich get richer" from interactions,[25] meaning that positive effects of using the Internet accrue to extroverts and those with social support but not to everyone. In a digital world filled with influencers who appear to be popular and successful, is there a negative impact on those receiving their messages, and is the effect so harmful that it is detrimental to the well-being of the larger society? The phrase "Fear of Missing Out" or FOMO may have always been a part of society, but perfectly staged Instagram photos and stunningly choreographed TikTok posts hold the potential to raise anxiety and exploit fears with direct product solutions.[26]

There is a concern regarding parasocial relationships in influencer marketing. This happens when an individual has the illusion that a relationship (here with an online influencer) is personal and reciprocal, when this is likely not the case.[27] Parasocial relationships have been identified in research as positively influencing both purchase activity and electronic word of mouth.[28] Unfortunately, it is often those with low self-esteem, who develop influential parasocial relationships. Other research has shown that social anxiety and parasocial relationships with YouTubers predict YouTube addiction (or maladaptive behaviors).[29]

Well-being is also being questioned for the products promoted. For example, research on children aged 9–10 years finds that when they watch an influencer promoting unhealthy snacks, they not only subsequently eat unhealthy snacks, but also they eat more overall.[30] Another major concern is the spread of misinformation on an array of health-related topics from tobacco and alcohol consumption to anti-vaccine and unvetted therapy promotion.[31] It is not only misinformation but also omitted information that could be potentially dangerous. When Kim Kardashian was paid $5,000,000 to promote Diclegis, a morning sickness drug, during her pregnancy, she did not post the side effects and was subsequently reprimanded by the FTC.[32]

Societal well-being may be eroded by the ever-widening gap in wealth exhibited on social media. On the one hand, celebrity and high-net-worth macro influencers are a fascination to many, but on the other hand, regular viewing of unattainable lifestyles can influence one's perception of reality. Just as with television, social media can repeatedly present a world that creates a socially constructed reality for the viewers, one where more people drive expensive cars, buy expensive clothes, and live in expensive houses than they actually do.[33] In order to make their extreme wealth palatable, researchers have found that high-net-worth individuals work to construct a persona that allows them to communicate with their followers.[34] Via interviews and examination of Instagram posts, these researchers found that the wealthy use three enacted personas, that of ambassador of "true" luxury, altruist, or "good" role model.[35]

## Social Trust

The 2016 U.S. presidential campaign and election brought social trust and, in particular, trust in social media into question. Typically, high trust is associated with societies where citizens believe there are few social conflicts and high public safety.[36] Social strife in the U.S. contributed to the overall skepticism of online communications. Future work to understand influence must address the trust that individuals hold in systems.

Media agency UM tracked more than 56,000 active Internet users across 81 countries to learn that only 8 percent of people believe that the bulk of information shared on social media is accurate and that only 4 percent agree that what influencers share is true.[37] Jess Markwood, from influencer marketing agency The Fifth, in discussing the future of influencers, argues that there should be a two-way street, one that offers mutual benefits, honesty, integrity (representing brands with shared values), trust, and loyalty[38] —in short, all the things one would want in a relationship. She suggests that influencers should document their transparency. As noted in Chapter 7, both influencers and brands can use analytical tools to help create and manage that relationship.

## Transitions and Substitutions

Although there is no clear dividing line between the endorser and the influencer, there is a general tendency to think of endorsers as being renowned for a skill or talent and then being sought after for an endorsement. In contrast, influencers build renown by communicating a skill or talent that guides, helps, or informs others. Is the future of influencer marketing about a transition from celebrity to micro and nano influencers? If trust-building organic influencers are the future, there could be a transition period that supports the expansion of marketing through small-scale influence.

Looking into the future, it seems likely that social media budgets will continue to grow and will likely draw from other existing marketing communications. Will this be taken from other digital budgets, from traditional advertising, from sponsorship and brand placement? Sponsorship and influencer marketing work well together, but there is the potential for leveraging of sponsored events and activities that currently go into advertising to be redirected to social media influencers.

## Managing Influencers

Another perspective on the future comes from those agencies that manage influencers. Researchers interviewed 19 U.S. advertising agency professionals about this uncharted territory and offered a number of observations (summarized here) about managing influencers into the future.[39]

- The cost of influencers is high, and managing these costs into the future is an open question.
- Contracts and legal fees are another expense but seen as important in achieving compliance with FTC rules.
- Agencies find it challenging to fit the creative freedom of influencers into their traditional structure, raising the question of who should be responsible for looking after them.
- Agencies also find vetting influencers, choosing those with whom to work, and overseeing their creative development to be challenging.
- From the agency side, the development of content is seen as a dance for influencers to maintain their own voices while also properly representing brands and their messages.
- Challenges remain in how best to measure the success of impressions and engagement coming from the influencer.

## Areas for Future Study

After reviewing the academic research on brand communications in social media, Hilde Voorveld from the Netherlands offered areas for future research,[40] which are summarized as questions here:

- How might social media influencers be understood in comparison with other forms of endorsement, and might characteristics such as their demographic similarity to those they influence uniquely influence response by consumers?
- What are the types of personalization in branded content, profiles, or hashtags, which influencers use, and how effective are they?
- What are the hidden persuasive intentions of social media, and how might consumers be empowered to resist or cope with persuasion attempts?

- What might be learned by researching a diverse set of social media platform characteristics?
- How might we better understand overall brand communications by better understanding the integration of social media in the overall media mix and the consumer's journey?

We can add the following questions for future researchers.

- Is there a path back from a crisis of trust, and, if so, how might an influencer repair reputation?
- What can an influencer do to establish and maintain authenticity?
- How might influencer marketing be moved in-house for brands through the use of employee brand ambassadors and CEOs?
- How can brands gauge the effect of interactivity in a creative influencer campaign?
- Could methods be developed that would isolate short-term values from long-term values of engaging influencers?
- What alternatives to followership or what composite indicators might be imagined for the selection of influencers?
- How will influencers develop in small business, business-to-business, education, and services such as healthcare?
- In addition to ROI, how could measures such as Return on Purpose (ROP) or Return on Engagement (ROE) be utilized in influencer marketing?

## The Near Future of Practice

In a number of spaces, there are new ways in which influencer marketing may be employed. We consider six here: globalization, crisis management, virtual influencers, diversity and inclusion, networking, in-house influencers, and sustainability.

### Globalization

With the global nature of social media, brands continue to look for influencers who can overcome cross-cultural and language barriers. People like Australian beauty influencer Shani Grimmond or Italian influencer Chiara Ferragni have shown that brands are interested in connecting with people whose popularity crosses borders.

### Crisis Management

In a very specific way, crisis management and influencer marketing may intersect when a brand experiences a breach in data security or a privacy violation. To have people who can shield the brand or talk convincingly about brand actions to mitigate risk means brands have to plan in advance.[41] More generally, in terms of addressing crises arising outside the firm, influencers are able to immediately change the tone of their content in far less time than traditional forms of advertising, which can be important in presenting the brand as responsive to issues as they arise.

### Virtual Influencers

Technology is also delivering virtual influencer personas. These computer-generated influencers such as imma.gram, a pink haired avatar created by Japanese firm ModelingCafe that has contracts with brands, including Puma, Valentino, and Dior Makeup, are becoming popular.[42] Another remarkable entry in this expanding category is a young avatar version of KFC's Colonel Sanders who tells the story of his entrepreneurial adventures.[43] He has a white suit, swank style, and has been featured with imma.gram. As more people have experiences with avatars in gaming, their visual acceptance, and even their created back stories, are becoming a part of the influencer marketing landscape. The clear advantage for marketers here is control and virtual influencers are expected to expand in scope.

### Diversity and Inclusion

Influencers can help a brand in communicating about their company and human resource strategies for representation. In fact, some influencers may actually lead these policies through their refusal to work with brands that do not have matching values in terms of representation.[44] That said, influencer marketing as a whole has been criticized for the lack of diversity.[45]

### Networking

Just as the young Colonel Sanders meets up with the pink-haired imma.gram, so too are other influencers working in tandem with the goal of supporting each other's popularity. Networking in influencer marketing began behind the scenes as marketers developed a portfolio. These networks are now regularly employed to support a focal influencer or celebrity.

### In-House Influencers

Employees are the next big wave of influencers. Brand ambassadors from within the ranks of companies have already become a mainstay for the brand voice, but to develop and support their social media content is another step toward in-house influencers. This may come from those closest to the product or service or from the CEO in the form of thought leadership.[46] Like virtual influencers, in-house influencers offer a degree of control for a brand.[47]

## Sustainability

In truth, we are all influencers, in what we say and do. Online and offline, each person holds the potential to sway others. A recent study finds that affluent individuals, particularly consumers in the global North, drive biophysical resource use (a) directly through high consumption, (b) as members of the capitalist class, and (c) through driving consumption norms across the population.[48] From unnecessary foods and flights to oversized homes and vehicles, the affluent communicate social norms. It is, however, the case that individuals are influencers based on their relative economic standing. In communities, looking to others to understand social norms is common.

The reality is that influencer marketing may be in a protracted state of evolution. The resistance of some to government guidelines and requirements of disclosure may be misguided. Confidence in influencers and what they say and why they say it is essential. Clearing up the motivations for influencer posts and comments might just make the entire industry more believable.

## Discussion Questions

1. Does the future of influencer marketing rely on social media, or do you think it will expand to the digital channels of other media (such as streamed TV or digital audio)?
2. Which influencers do you think have—or could have—a global presence? What makes them (or could make them) effective globally?
3. Consider a brand that has faced a public relations crisis (such as PriceWaterhouseCoopers handing the announcer the wrong envelope for Best Picture at the 2018 Academy Awards, or when Woke Up Like This makeup brand decided to name a blusher, "Dream Like Anne" to honor genocide victim, Anne Frank). How might an influencer have helped in each situation? Is there a specific influencer you would recommend, and why?
4. Which virtual influencers do you follow and/or find interesting? How does their influence compare to that of a human influencer?
5. Influencer marketing has been criticized for a lack of diversity. Is this a general phenomenon or does it differ depending on the product category?

6. Should all companies expect their employees to act as brand ambassadors? How can companies use these people most effectively in influencer marketing?

## Notes

1. www.businessinsider.com/influencer-marketing-report
2. www.stuff.co.nz/entertainment/celebrities/113598705/the-instagram-backlash-influencers-who-lost-their-influence
3. www.socialmediatoday.com/news/why-the-future-of-influencer-marketing-will-be-organic-influencers/567463/
4. www.hollywoodreporter.com/live-feed/five-years-network-ratings-declines-explained-1241524
5. www.statista.com/statistics/910875/us-most-popular-video-streaming-services-by-monthly-average-users/
6. https://techcrunch.com/2020/02/20/twitch-to-top-40-million-u-s-viewers-next-year-forecast-says/
7. https://techcrunch.com/2020/02/20/twitch-to-top-40-million-u-s-viewers-next-year-forecast-says/
8. Nielsen Streaming TV Update, April 2020.
9. www.marketingcharts.com/digital/social-media-108342
10. www.bloomberg.com/news/articles/2019-11-30/what-the-streaming-wars-mean-for-the-future-of-tv-quicktake
11. https://blog.beatly.com/en/blog/ai-influencers-future-influencer-marketing
12. www.wsj.com/articles/the-making-of-a-computer-generated-influencer-11544702401
13. www.usatoday.com/story/life/2019/10/16/cgi-influencers-blur-line-between-reality-and-fantasy-instagram-advertising/3790471002/
14. Toffler, A. (1980). *The third wave.* New York: Bantam Books.
15. Næss, H. E., & Tickell, S. (2019). Fan engagement in motorsports: A case of the FIA world rally championship. *The Journal of Media Innovations, 5*(1), 31–44.
16. www.aperto.com/en/work/volkswagen-wrc
17. https://static1.squarespace.com/static/5b1f2ba0b40b9d244893933e/t/5e83608cc927de74e8d5d298/1585668329525/Trends+Report+The+Impact+of+Coronavirus+on+Influencer+Marketing+Obviously.pdf
18. Dumont, G. (2017). The beautiful and the damned: The work of new media production in professional rock climbing. *Journal of Sport and Social Issues, 41*(2), 99–117.
19. Dumont, G. (2018). Creativity at work: The production of work for sale by brand ambassadors. *Journal of Cultural Economy, 11*(1), 69–82.
20. https://apnews.com/a059f16cba96ce115152b577a97e3ea6
21. https://themasb.org/sponsorship-accountability-pt-9-nili/
22. De Veirman, M., Hudders, L., & Nelson, M. R. (2019). What is influencer marketing and how does it target children? A review and direction for future research. *Frontiers in Psychology, 10*, 2685.
23. Qutteina, Y., Hallez, L., Mennes, N., De Backer, C., & Smits, T. (2019). What do adolescents see on social media? A diary study of food marketing images on social media. *Frontiers in Psychology, 10*, 2637.

24. Kraut, R., Patterson, M., Lundmark, V., Kiesler, S., Mukophadhyay, T., & Scherlis, W. (1998). Internet paradox: A social technology that reduces social involvement and psychological well-being? *American Psychologist, 53*(9), 1017.
25. Kraut, R., Kiesler, S., Boneva, B., Cummings, J., Helgeson, V., & Crawford, A. (2002). Internet paradox revisited. *Journal of Social Issues, 58*(1), 49–74.
26. www.cnet.com/how-to/how-marketers-use-social-media-fomo-to-sell-you-things-and-how-you-can-keep-your-money/
27. Horton, D., & Strauss, A. (1957). Interaction in audience participation shows. *The American Journal of Sociology, 62*, 579–587.
28. Hwang, K., & Zhang, Q. (2018). Influence of parasocial relationship between digital celebrities and their followers on followers' purchase and electronic word-of-mouth intentions, and persuasion knowledge. *Computers in Human Behavior, 87*, 155–173.
29. de Bérail, P., Guillon, M., & Bungener, C. (2019). The relations between YouTube addiction, social anxiety and parasocial relationships with YouTubers: A moderated-mediation model based on a cognitive-behavioral framework. *Computers in Human Behavior, 99*, 190–204.
30. Coates, A. E., Hardman, C. A., Halford, J. C., Christiansen, P., & Boyland, E. J. (2019). Social media influencer marketing and children's food intake: A randomized trial. *Pediatrics, 143*(4), e20182554.
31. Chou, W. Y. S., Oh, A., & Klein, W. M. (2018). Addressing health-related misinformation on social media. *Jama, 320*(23), 2417–2418.
32. Thomas, K. (2019). Key opinion leaders supercharged by the internet: Paid doctor and patient influencers on social media. *BMJ, 365*, 12336.
33. O'guinn, T. C., & Shrum, L. J. (1997). The role of television in the construction of consumer reality. *Journal of Consumer Research, 23*(4), 278–294.
34. Leban, M., Thomsen, T. U., von Wallpach, S., & Voyer, B. G. (2020). Constructing personas: How high-net-worth social media influencers reconcile ethicality and living a luxury lifestyle. *Journal of Business Ethics*, 1–15.
35. Ibid.
36. Delhey, J., & Newton, K. (2003). Who trusts? The origins of social trust in seven societies. *European Societies, 5*(2), 93–137.
37. www.thedrum.com/news/2019/05/09/only-4-people-trust-what-influencers-say-online
38. Markwood, J. (2019). What the future of influencer relationships should look like. *Talking Influence*. Retrieved from https://talkinginfluence.com/2019/05/13/what-the-future-of-influencer-relationships-should-look-like/
39. Childers, C. C., Lemon, L. L., & Hoy, M. G. (2019). # Sponsored# Ad: Agency perspective on influencer marketing campaigns. *Journal of Current Issues & Research in Advertising, 40*(3), 258–274.
40. Voorveld, H. A. (2019). Brand communication in social media: A research agenda. *Journal of Advertising, 48*(1), 14–26.
41. www.business2community.com/crisis-management/influencer-marketing-and-crisis-management-perfect-combination-in-a-storm-7-facts-to-consider-02146985
42. https://influencerdb.com/blog/top-10-virtual-influencers/
43. Ibid.
44. www.forbes.com/sites/katetalbot/2019/06/02/diversity-in-influencer-marketing-why-representation-matters/#18256197a3e6

45. www.adweek.com/brand-marketing/influencer-marketing-has-an-implicit-bias-problem/
46. https://dmexco.com/stories/thought-leader-marketing-the-ceo-becomes-an-influencer/
47. https://izea.com/2019/05/02/in-house-influencer-team/
48. Wiedmann, T., Lenzen, M., Keyßer, L. T., & Steinberger, J. K. (2020). Scientists' warning on affluence. *Nature Communications, 11*(1), 1–10.

## Further Reading

Boerman, S. C., & Van Reijmersdal, E. A. (2020). Disclosing influencer marketing on YouTube to children: The moderating role of para-social relationship. *Frontiers in Psychology, 10*, 3042.

O'Neill, E. E. (2019). Influencing the future: Compensating children in the age of social-media influencer marketing. *Stanford Law Review Online, 72*, 42.

Polo, M. P. (2020). The role of prosumers in the interactive and digital processes of public relations: The organisation of events and influencers as the new emerging stakeholder. In *Handbook of research on transmedia storytelling, audience engagement, and business strategies* (pp. 161–174). Hershey, PA: IGI Global.

Reinikainen, H., Munnukka, J., Maity, D., & Luoma-aho, V. (2020). "You really are a great big sister": Parasocial relationships, credibility, and the moderating role of audience comments in influencer marketing. *Journal of Marketing Management, 36*(3–4), 279–298.

Seeler, S., Lück, M., & Schänzel, H. A. (2019). Exploring the drivers behind experience accumulation: The role of secondary experiences consumed through the eyes of social media influencers. *Journal of Hospitality and Tourism Management, 41*, 80–89.

Sharma, R., Ahuja, V., & Alavi, S. (2018). The future scope of netnography and social network analysis in the field of marketing. *Journal of Internet Commerce, 17*(1), 26–45.

# INDEX

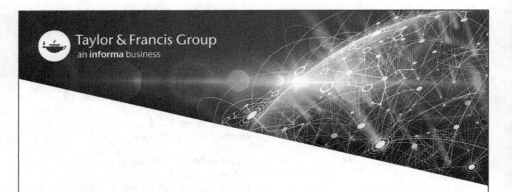